RECOVERING COMMON GOODS

Recovering Common Goods

Patrick Riordan SJ

VERITAS

Published 2017 by
Veritas Publications
7–8 Lower Abbey Street
Dublin 1
Ireland
publications@veritas.ie
www.veritas.ie

ISBN 978 1 84730 782 8

10 9 8 7 6 5 4 3 2 1

A catalogue record for this book is available from the British Library.

Designed by Padraig McCormack, Veritas Publications
Printed in Ireland by SPRINT-print Ltd, Dublin

*Veritas books are printed on paper made from the wood pulp of managed forests.
For every tree felled, at least one tree is planted, thereby renewing natural resources.*

Table of Contents

Introduction

This book is about our common goods. I've been writing about this topic for many years, but mostly within the academic discipline of political philosophy. Studying and teaching political philosophy, I came to realise that the important tradition of Catholic social thought made little impact on academic debates. Despite the wealth of experience, concern and analysis gathered in the Church's traditions, professionals in the disciplines of politics and philosophy, at least in the English-speaking world, did not take Catholic social thought seriously. There are many reasons for this, as we can imagine. My main interest was to recover the riches of the Catholic intellectual heritage and make this heritage accessible for contemporary students and thinkers. In particular, I focused on the concept of common good. The literature in ethics and politics largely avoids the topic of the good, since it is assumed that there can be no agreement on the good in a pluralist world and a pluralist · society. Each person is assumed to have their own notion of what is good for them, and while it might happen that many people could agree on what they want, inevitably there will be many others who do not agree, and so the basis for a shared political order will not be a common view of the good. In order to challenge this widespread, and in my view naïve, assumption I wrote a book entitled *A Politics of the Common Good* (Dublin: Institute of Public Administration, 1996) in which I argued that a philosophy of liberal politics needs a concept of common goods. Having made the case for the usefulness of the concept and language of common goods, I went on to explore what exactly could and could not be said using this language. This led to another book, *A Grammar of the Common Good* (London: Continuum, 2008) in which I laid out the strengths as well as the limitations of common good language. The reluctance of my colleagues in philosophy and political science to use the concept of common good was partly due to the vagueness of the notion and the way it might be used to say nothing while appearing to say a lot. I was particularly sensitive to this concern, since I recognised that bishops and other preachers and Church leaders often invoke the common good in a pious way, but manage to say nothing at all of help in concrete situations. Our world is full of conflicts and we can observe that many individuals and groups pursue their own interests, and we might wish that the common good would prevail. But what would that entail? What does that tell us about the right thing to do? For instance, in industrial disputes, in which trades unions representing the interests of workers either strike or threaten strikes, it is clear that there is a conflict of interests between employers and workers. Many others can be badly affected, as in the case of transport disruptions, for instance. Church leaders might appeal to everyone to consider the common good. But what does that mean? Are the workers to give in and allow the employers have their way? Or are the employers and owners of business to give in to the demands of workers? Appealing to the common good does not actually help in the concrete case since it does not give directions as to the correct or best resolution of the dispute. In fact, the value and richness of the concept of common good can be undermined by its uncritical application by well-meaning commentators who wish for peace. That is why I thought it important to work out exactly what can and cannot be said using the language of the common good. The argument was addressed not only to philosophers and other academics who were sceptical of the value of this language; it was also addressed to theologians and Church authorities who were perhaps too enthusiastic but uncritical in their appeal to common goods.

I was in Boston in the fateful year of 9/11 (2001–2) and observed the reaction of the American people and their leaders to the dreadful attacks on New York, Washington and Pennsylvania. The notion of common good was invoked again and again, understandably, as people rallied together to find comfort and support in each other's presence. The sense of solidarity with the victims was strong: everyone had stories of friends or relatives who were close to the twin towers or who knew someone who was, or who narrowly escaped being affected. There was a tangible sense that everyone was a victim, that the whole country had been attacked and that the national response brought everyone together. Not surprising then that people spoke about the common good and used it as a slogan to invoke and strengthen the sense of national unity. Along with everyone else present in the country at that time, I was caught up in the communal pain and anxiety of Americans, but I did wonder if the common good in that case was identical with the good of the United States of America and its citizens alone. What about the rest of the world? What about the Islamic countries and peoples: do we share common goods with them? What about peoples divided by war and conflict of interest: can they be said to have goods in common, despite the conflict? What else might the common good be other than national self-interest? This line of thought led to my next book, *Global Ethics and Global Common Goods* (London: Bloomsbury, 2015) in which I tried to spell out the full range of application of common goods, stretching from very particular forms of cooperation, over local and national communities, to the international and global level, to humanity as a whole.

In this book, *Recovering Common Goods*, I revisit these discussions but reframe them in a new way for a different audience. To date my work has been academic, and it is addressed to practitioners, whether professionals in academia or in government or in the human sciences. As such, it has tried to anticipate challenges and criticisms which might arise against the background of long-running debates, for instance about the sources of obligation or the bases of political authority. In my previous books, I have maintained a purely academic approach, confining my arguments to what might be acceptable in philosophy. Arguments presented had to rely only on reasons and analysis available to everyone: there could be no appeal to authority, or revelation or Church teaching. At the same time, I have not concealed my motivation for this work, which is rooted in my Catholic faith and Jesuit priesthood. I have wanted to present and elaborate the intellectual heritage of the Catholic tradition, which I see as a resource and a treasure for all of humankind. It is to be put at the service of the ongoing human search for a way of life which is commensurate with the dignity of every human being and that enables each one in freedom to pursue their fulfilment.

I believe that the analysis and clarification that has been achieved in philosophy should be available to everyone and that is the task I set myself in writing this book. Here, I focus on and address people who are engaged in their local communities and who are activists in charitable organisations and other civil society organisations, or who are simply citizens who want to exercise their civic responsibilities in ways that resonate with their baptismal vocation to be Christians in the world. I think, for instance, of the hundreds of delegates to the annual meeting of the Justice and Peace and Integrity of Creation Network, whom I met and addressed on the common good. These are people from parishes throughout England and Wales who work tirelessly in their local communities for justice and peace, and, most recently, with the concern for the integrity of creation. I would like to make my work available to them and to many like them. In taking this on I will be explicit about my faith motivation, but more than that: I will attempt to link the philosophical analysis with reflections on the gospels and sacred scripture as well as with the great range of material that is to be found in Catholic social thought. I acknowledge that what I offer is my own personal attempt to make sense of what I do as a believer and a Jesuit priest, and to explain how I see the philosophical analysis that I do on the day job as contributing to the mission which the Lord has given his Church. What I personally have found encouraging and nurturing for my own faith is the repeated experience that progress in the secular philosophical analysis has always also been a discovery of the depth and richness of the gospel and its promises. One example, which will be explored at greater length in a later chapter, is how I have come to understand the concept of common good not as empty and vague, but as open and programmatic, naming something we are still in the process of discovering. But how could it be otherwise? Isn't the promise of something 'which no eye has yet seen nor ear heard', something beyond our wildest dreams and imaginings, the good that God has prepared for his people? (1 Cor 2:9)

This is a personal account of my motivation and inspiration for the positions I have taken up in the course of my work. It is presented in the hope that it will be helpful for people who are shaping their own practical commitments and reflecting on their reasons for those commitments. I try to keep the academic toolbox to a minimum, with as few references as possible. Where it might be helpful, I point to sources that readers might wish to consult and to relevant further reading. There is no attempt to be exhaustive.

I realise that some readers will be disappointed that I do not address some current concerns that they might like to see explored in a book on the common good. There are issues concerning law and morality once again fuelling heated public debate in Ireland. I think of the campaign to repeal the eighth amendment to the constitution and the recent legalisation of same-sex marriage. I do not enter into these debates in this book, because I want to concentrate on elaborating the notion of common good, and to make that analysis available to all parties in current disputes. I would hope that the positions I take up are consistent with what I write here about common goods. For reflections on the relationship between Catholic Church teaching and public morality, I refer readers to my articles in *Studies* as follows: 'Can we not Discuss Morals?', *Studies*, 80 (1991), pp. 377–87; 'Abortion: The Aftermath of the Supreme Court's Decision', *Studies*, 81 (1992), pp. 293–302; 'Public Order: The Embryo' in E. McDonagh and V. MacNamara (eds), *An Irish Reader in Moral Theology: The Legacy of the Last Fifty Years, Vol. III: Medical and Bio Ethics*, Dublin: Columba Press, 2013, pp. 207–15; 'Irish Experiments in Living' in *Studies*, 102 (2013), pp. 149–58; 'The Purpose of the Law: The Case of Same-sex Marriage' in *Studies*, 103 (2014), pp. 10–19.

Chapter One
A Good Laugh

The ability to tell amusing stories and share jokes with eloquence and fluency is often considered a gift. It can unite a disparate group and help break the ice; it can also bring a community together. The presence of a person with the gift of the gab, a seanchaí or a raconteur is a bonus for any gathering – bringing people together and making them laugh is an example of a shared joy and a common good. The experience of hearing an amusing tale or anecdote also widens the circle because people in the gathering are drawn to the group that is sharing joy and laughter. A witty person can bring a spark of fun to ordinary conversation and enliven any group and rightly earn the Dubliner's praise: 'Sharp as a blade, quick as lightning, like a rapier on the comeback. A gift for the repartee!'

Laughter is definitely therapeutic. Especially if we can laugh at ourselves, it helps us to get things in perspective and to manage challenges and crises that might otherwise overwhelm us. But laughter, like song, lifts us out of ourselves and enables us to turn our attention to a wider reality. Some philosophers have explored this line of thought, focusing on humour, the ability to laugh, as a distinctively human characteristic.

There is a characteristic sense of humour among Irish people, and I become aware of it when abroad in different cultures, where people are unable to distinguish between what is serious and what is fun in what we say. Sometimes words and expressions as well as timing are crucial to delivering a punchline and often meaning can simply get lost in translation.

The English comedy actor John Cleese once told the story of recording an episode of the television series *Fawlty Towers*, which was always recorded before a live audience. On one occasion the gags were all falling flat, nobody was laughing, the audience sat still and attentive but without reacting, and the actors were growing more and more anxious about the material and their performance. Was it really not funny at all? At a break they discovered the reason: the audience that night was a tourist group from Iceland, who, while they might have enough English to get by, certainly didn't have enough to understand the peculiar humour typical of the programme. How difficult it must have been for the performers, without any reaction from the audience!

Have you ever been part of a group of people enjoying themselves, telling entertaining stories and swapping jokes, but you feel left out because somehow or other you don't understand? Perhaps they are speaking a language that you are just learning, so you don't understand enough to see the point, or perhaps the stories all refer to some area of work experience that is foreign to you. You've found yourself thrown among a group of lawyers laughing hilariously at some anecdotes, for instance, but their stories presuppose familiarity with the technicalities of the law, so you don't know what they're talking about. To be present but not included: that is hell. A very unpleasant experience, in that we are made painfully aware of our exclusion from the group, but it also makes us aware of the deep desire to belong, to be a member of the community sharing in the joy and fun.

This is another aspect of the joke-telling and sharing an amusing story experience worth analysing further. A community is created by the narration of the story. Not a very intense or deep community, and possibly short-lived, but nonetheless real. We find ourselves united in being interested in hearing the story and how it ends; in a noisy pub you can see how the heads lean in to catch what is being said. And when the punchline is delivered we are united in the explosion of laughter, and we enjoy the joke all the more in seeing that our fellows are also enjoying it immensely. Isn't it perhaps this absence of company that makes the solitary and silent reading of funny stories less entertaining than hearing the same stories told in a group of friends?

There's a wonderful scene in G.K. Chesterton's 'Ballad of the White Horse'. King Alfred has been struck in the face by an old woman because while left to mind the fire he had allowed her cakes to burn. His first reaction is anger, but then he laughs at himself. The powerful king stops himself from striking the old woman just in time. Instead of an appeal to dignity, to his wounded pride, he suddenly recognises what a ridiculous figure he makes. And Chesterton notes in the poem what a strange thing this is, 'one man laughing at himself'. This is at the heart of a Christian appreciation of comedy that can poke fun at humankind without falling into the attitude of contempt for others: 'tales that … end not all in scorning'. At the heart of humour is love.

> The giant laughter of Christian men
> That roars through a thousand tales,

Where greed is an ape and pride is an ass,
And Jack's away with his master's lass,
And the miser is banged with all his brass,
The farmer with all his flails;

Tales that tumble and tales that trick,
Yet end not all in scorning –
Of kings and clowns in a merry plight,
And the clock gone wrong and the world gone right,
That the mummers sing upon Christmas night
And Christmas Day in the morning.

This experience of storytelling provides me with a useful example to explore what is meant by a common good. It allows us to identify several different but related goods in common, so that we can see how the concept can be applied in a range of meanings. In the experience of sharing a joke or an entertaining story we have a group of people united in the enjoyment of something in which they delight, which they would not want to have missed, and which they had desired in paying close attention to the narrative. That which they enjoy is a good in common: the fun, the understanding of the punchline and the grasp of the whole. But that moment of shared enjoyment and shared appreciation of the wit and humour is not the only good in common. The community itself, the group, brought together by the shared experience, is also a common good shared by the participants. The sense of humour that enables each of the members to share in the fun is also a resource for all together: without it, the group could not enjoy the company of others, essential for the experience. Another good in common is the occasion and the opportunity to be together and to have fun;

while such occasions can occur spontaneously, they are usually the result of someone taking the trouble to organise the event and bring people together.

This reflection on the joke-telling experience can be taken further and applied to an understanding of the ultimate goods in common. The telling of a story creates a community; the community presupposes a shared sense of humour; the community's enjoyment of the story occurs in the appreciation of the point, the punchline. Can this be used as an analogy to understand what is going on in revelation? God the Father is telling a story, through the work of creation and through revelation in the scriptures and especially in the gospels. The Son is the Word, the point of it all, for whom and through whom all things were made. God the Son, entered into human history, has become part of the story and indeed has become the point of the story which we call Good News, gospel. It is a delightful, beautiful story, which invites our enjoyment. The Holy Spirit is the sense of humour in the listeners to the story, which enables them to understand and enjoy what they are hearing. Without this gift we are at a loss and completely unable to enter into the spirit of the tale. Also, those who listen and appreciate the story are bonded together in a community of enjoyment and celebration, which gives us an analogy for Church, the community of those who have the Spirit enabling them to receive the Word and treasure it in their hearts. This analogy gives us another clarification about the difference between time and eternity, this life and the next. In time, in history, there is a sequence of events, as in the telling of a story. The elements of the story or joke are laid out, step by step, one after the other, building up the tension and the expectation and wonder how it will all end. Finally, with the delivery of the punchline or the dramatic point of the entertaining tale, there is an explosion of laughter in a single moment as all the elements are finally grasped in their unity, contributing to the meaning of the point. This is the analogy for eternity: not an endless continuation and repetition of the same, but a single moment in which all the elements of meaning are grasped and enjoyed. That would be heaven, an existence beyond time, but in which all time is grasped in its entirety. As hinted above, hell by contrast would be exclusion – presence without inclusion, without participation, not because anyone is actually excluding you, but because you lack the Spirit of humour and fail to see the Truth of the Good News story.

With this reflection on the divine narrative we have further meanings for common goods, being the goods of community in the enjoyment of God's self-communication. The ultimate common good is God himself, the source of all goodness. But to appreciate this we need to reflect further on what is meant by good. We'll explore this some more in the next chapter. But here I want to enquire further about the meaning of good, and common good, in relation to morality understood as rules and regulations. When we say that something is good, does that mean that we are saying it is a duty to pursue the good or to act to bring it about? This is a frequent enough misunderstanding of what is meant by common good. People are irritated by being told what is their common good, because they interpret the identification of the common good as the imposition of an obligation to act for the identified good.

Relying on the example of joke or storytelling, we can see easily enough the misunderstanding involved in thinking that there are rules and duties involved when we identify it as a common good. Would it make sense to instruct people that they ought to have a sense of humour, and that they ought to laugh at a good joke? How would people react if they were instructed to enjoy their friends' company? Nobody has to be told that they ought to enjoy a good story and good company; they already do and wish to do precisely that. We do it because we are attracted by the good; we are enticed into the circle by the prospect of the kind of enjoyment that delights us. The good attracts. We don't have to be driven towards it.

Throughout history lawmakers have attempted to regulate comical entertainments and forbid mockery of the authorities, both in the Church and in the state. In 1254 the question was debated to what extent the civil law ought to curb the output of artists who mocked the religious and royal authorities. King Louis IX – the only French king to have been canonised as a saint – understood his royal authority in theological terms, considering it his duty to enforce the moral and religious teachings of scripture and the Church. He applied the law as an instrument of moral education. He introduced laws to suppress the mockery of royal and religious persons and institutions. Laws promulgated by him also prohibited: cursing, swearing, blasphemy, games of chance and gambling, and attempted to abolish various vices, including usury and prostitution.

At the time of this legislation Thomas Aquinas was at the University in Paris, living in the Dominican Priory of St Jacques – Louis IX was a benefactor of the priory. Some years later, Aquinas wrote on the question whether the civil law should prohibit all the vices. The questions he addressed were not hypothetical, but were rooted in the experience of those earlier years when he had actually seen a civil power that regarded as its duty the stamping out of bad behaviour.

There is a contrast between their reasoning. Louis IX's motivation had been good and his ambition had been praiseworthy: that all his subjects would be morally faultless. Aquinas objected to the use of civil law to effect the moral perfection of the king's subjects. On his understanding of the role of law and of civil authority in making law, its function is oriented to the common good of public order, and not to the moral perfection of people. Where Louis IX appeals to Christian theological arguments, Aquinas argues from natural reason, generating standards that should apply to all rulers, whether Christian or not.

Two questions posed by Aquinas in his Compendium of Theology, the *Summa Theologiae*, highlight the contrast to the French King. He asks first whether human law should forbid all morally wrong actions. His account of morality relies on an understanding of the virtues, such as justice and temperance, charity and mercy. Immoral actions then are not virtuous, but vicious, for instance an expression of vice. Care must be taken not to confuse the present understanding of 'vice' with that relied on by Aquinas. His answer is short and precise:

> human law is framed for a number of human beings, the majority of whom are not perfect in virtue. Wherefore, human laws do not forbid all vices from which the virtuous abstain but only the more grievous vices from which it is possible for the majority to abstain and chiefly those that are to the hurt of others, without the prohibition of which human society could not be maintained; thus human law prohibits murder, theft, and suchlike. (*ST*, IIa IIae, q. 96, a. 2)

In other words, the lawmaker's concern is with the preservation of society and its good order.

Aquinas mentions only two examples (but suggests there are others) for the kind of behaviour that threatens public order: murder and theft. Murder violates the good of life; theft violates the good of property. If these goods were not secured, social life would be impossible. It is fascinating to see Aquinas anticipating this very modern concern to limit the scope of action of civil authorities in relation to the behaviour of citizens.

Aquinas's emphasis on the social function of human-made law as distinct from a potential moral perfectionist purpose is evident in his discussion of the parallel question, whether human law should command acts of all the virtues. His answer is that:

> [L]aw is ordained to the common good. Wherefore, there is no virtue whose acts cannot be prescribed by the law. Nevertheless, human law does not prescribe concerning all the acts of every virtue but only in regard to those that are ordained to the common good – either immediately, as when certain things are done directly for the common good, or mediately, as when a lawgiver prescribes certain things pertaining to good training whereby the citizens are disciplined in the upholding of the common good of justice and peace. (*ST*, IIa IIae, q. 96, a. 3)

No dimension of human behaviour is ruled out, since anything can have an impact on the goods of social order. And so it is conceivable that the civil lawmaker would attempt to regulate this or that behaviour to the extent that it is significant for good public order.

Aquinas sees two kinds of situation, one in which the impact on public order is indirect, as for instance in the regulation of educational standards by which the authorities attempt to ensure that all are sufficiently equipped to exercise their responsibilities as citizens. In the other case the impact is immediate. An obvious example is the requirement in some democracies that all citizens exercise their duty to vote, or that all take their turn in doing jury service. It is the common good of public order that explains why this or another action is made obligatory by the law. In our context, all have moral obligations to share from their abundance with those who are poor, but this moral duty is not enforced in the civil law. Or at least, the share of taxation which goes towards supporting the health and welfare and education systems – goods which can also be appreciated in terms of public order – does not exhaust the moral obligations of the wealthy to share their wealth. These themes of the direct and indirect contributions to the common good will recur in later chapters when we consider the economy, democracy and education in terms of common goods.

Louis IX was not alone in attempting to outlaw subversive public entertainment: the Pope had done likewise in his dominions, as had the Emperor Frederick II in Naples. But Aquinas, who along with his fellow Dominicans in Paris had been a target of a mocking ballad and had experienced also the effects of attempts to enforce the law against balladeers, was prepared to see the positive contribution that such performers make to social life. In discussing play as activity undertaken for the sake of its own pleasure, Aquinas acknowledges a positive function for fun and games, including the entertainment provided by minstrels, and he recognises this as legitimate occupation (*ST*, IIa IIae, q. 168). Hence, for Aquinas, a society without wandering entertainers, or their functional equivalent, would be a defective society, one defective in respect of achievement of its common good. The common good requires the making of jokes and the staging and enjoyment of entertainments. His focus is on the shared enjoyment of important goods rather than on the potential or actual misuse of human capacities.

It is ironic that the Dominican priest upholds the human and social values at stake in the debate, while the civil authority with which he disagrees appeals to religious and theological arguments. Yes, the authority in question was a holy man, later canonised by the Church, but from Aquinas's point of view he misunderstood the function of law and of the civil authority he was called upon to exercise.

In our twenty-first-century context it is hardly conceivable that such an issue might be addressed without recourse to the language of human rights. In particular, appeal might be made to the freedom of expression, the human right to the freedom of speech. Even if that language were available to him, Aquinas does not have to appeal to human rights. He can present his case in terms of the goods at stake, and the contrast between different kinds of good, and the corresponding duties or responsibilities in relation to them. On the one hand, there is the good which is the moral fulfilment or flourishing of persons. On the other hand, there is the public good of order, and the maintenance of a society in which it is possible for people to have the conditions necessary for them to pursue their more ultimate goods. As noted above, the good of social order will require the protection of more specific goods, such as human life and property. But also as noted above, the good of social order will require too that spaces are secured in which the shared enjoyment of human goods of pleasure and entertainment can take place. Corresponding to these different kinds of goods are sets of duties. Aquinas leaves no one in doubt about a person's duty to do what is right, seen from the perspective of his or her fulfilment or holiness. But in his discussion of the texts above he is making the point that it is not the obligation of the civil lawmaker to look primarily to the moral fulfilment of citizens, but rather the obligation is towards the goods of public order. It will always be a matter of prudential judgement as to what in any particular situation will damage or benefit public order. So it is not unreasonable that different jurisdictions will take a variety of approaches to matters for legislation, accommodating the law to the particular circumstances and characters of people.

Chapter Two
Goods and Values

The image of a group of friends enjoying an entertaining story together gave us a helpful example to understand something about common goods. Other examples will be helpful in answering questions often raised about common goods. For instance, people wonder why we need to talk about common goods when we can talk about values, especially shared values. But is there a difference between a good and a value, and do we need different terms? Are things said to be good because we value them, so that the real question is not about things that are valued, but about the people who desire them? And if we want to argue for the idea that some things simply are good, does it follow that people have to value them in the sense of being obliged to desire or choose or pursue them? These are the kinds of questions raised by people who fear that talk of common goods will result in having someone else's view of their good imposed on them so that they are ultimately deprived of freedom in their choice of lifestyle. It may seem a bit fussy to bother about the terms and definitions, but actually it can be very helpful for dealing with real concerns like those above to have a clear idea of what we can say and what we can defend, and at the same time identify the problems we might expect.

Wherever people work together to achieve something they have a common project, a goal in common. For example, for a football team it might be the championship trophy; for parents it might be a campaign to get a new school for their children. There are many different ways in which people work together, and for any one person he or she will be involved in many different groups and organisations, collaborating for different objectives – every one of these might give us examples for understanding common goods. Even for any one person who attempted to make a list of all their involvements, with family and neighbours, with work colleagues, clients, suppliers and customers, pastime activities such as sports, hobbies, participation in politics both local and national, and Church affiliation, the list would be very long indeed. And these examples above are not exhaustive. Nothing has been mentioned about education or healthcare. People visit the doctor and dentist, opticians and pharmacists, and may be involved with hospitals or nursing homes.

There is a tendency to want to simplify because of the complexity and variety of examples of working together as a common good. So we might resort to the kind of abstraction, which is common in social sciences such as economics or sociology. Instead of considering the great range of human goods and purposes, we try to simplify by looking away from this variety of activities and look instead at the actor who is engaged in these activities. That's what economics does: relies on a model that supposes that everyone has desires and preferences and that they use their reason to work out how they can get what they want. The model assumes that rational people are bargain hunters, always looking for the best deal. This analysis abstracts from the great variety of things that people actually pursue. But it is too simple to say that people want to satisfy their desires in the most cost-effective way possible. The model stresses that reason's role is to ensure effectiveness and efficiency, but reason has nothing to contribute to forming people's wants and desires. These are simply given, what people happen to desire. There is some usefulness in having such a simplified model of choice because it enables the generation of hypotheses and theories that can be tested empirically. It contributes a lot to making sociology and economics into social sciences. The great disadvantage is that people forget the abstract theorising involved in building such a model, and take the model as a reliable description of what actual choices and decisions are like. Some people even go further and claim that a person *should* use this model as a guide to their own action to ensure it is rational.

This involves a dreadful distortion of human reality. On the one hand, it encourages people to think exclusively in terms of self-interest – asking themselves before every decision whether they are getting a good deal. This way of thinking makes people reluctant to commit to anything, since they are always waiting in hope of a better offer. On the other hand, it blinds people to what is really going on in forms of cooperation and service all around them. The mindset shaped by rational choice theory looks on at carers who go out of their way to look after their charges. This mindset might assume that the people who act this way are just satisfying their own desires and acting out of their preferences, and so they are succeeding in getting what they want. Professionals often spoken of as following a vocation, in teaching, nursing and healthcare, therapy and Church ministry and politics can sometimes be deemed to be satisfying personal desires. One negative consequence of this view is the widespread assumption that people following a vocation don't need to be paid so much since they have other pay-offs.

A similar distortion arises in the understanding of business when the accountant's perspective is used. An accountant looks at a balance sheet, and checks the bottom line. Is the business losing or making money? A valid question, since it identifies a necessary condition for any business, that it not merely break even, but make money. The distortion arises when business is defined exclusively or primarily in terms of this necessary condition. That happens when the maximisation of shareholder value is taken as the point of business. Profit, return to investors is seen as the main objective. But this abstracts completely from the great range of goods and services provided by businesses. When you ask business people what they do, they rarely will speak of their bottom line, but tell you instead, often with pride, about the products they manufacture and market, or the services they provide to clients. These goods and services fit into the practical projects of other businesses, or of final consumers, allowing them to achieve their ambitions. The purposes of business are many and varied, and they correspond to the full range of human goods, so it is a distortion to interpret business simply in terms of the generation of profit or the return to shareholders.

Abstractions can become distortions, and we have noted two examples of that danger. The first is when we abstract from the many goods and projects that people pursue and focus on their motivation, their desires or preferences. The distortion comes when we reduce all motivation to one category, desire, and we assume in addition that people act to satisfy their desires.

The second example is when we abstract from the many goods and services provided by businesses and focus on the bottom line. The distortion comes when all products and services are reduced to one category, revenue, and we assume in addition that all entrepreneurs act for the sake of profit only. To avoid these distortions we make use of another abstraction which serves the purpose of directing our attention to the full range of goals that people pursue. Values are abstract, while goods are concrete. Values express the point of our activity and collaboration, by giving the sense of our many goals. The great range of goods involved in the many forms of collaboration from business to caring can be summarised under the notion of value.

If I were to ask shoppers in a supermarket what they are doing, they would wonder why I ask something so obvious and ordinary? Can't I see that they are doing the weekly shop? Though they might be buying food to prepare a meal; a meal together is always more than simply taking in food and drink, carbohydrates, vitamins and proteins, although these are important. It is an expression and a realisation of friendship, companionship and community. While the food on the table is specific and particular – it is potatoes not rice, parsnips not cabbage, cabernet sauvignon not merlot – the values at stake are formulated more abstractly. Nutrition, friendship, aesthetics, play, knowledge, religion and creativity are among the values that can be invoked to make sense of what is going on. In comparison with the meal on the table and the persons sitting down, the values are abstract, and some, such as nutrition, point to the further values of health and life. Values express the point of the activity and of the particular goods pursued in that activity. Strictly speaking, when we act, we act for some concrete specific good. Were the people in the supermarket to answer my naïve questions they would give definite concrete answers. They are buying this bread and not that, these vegetables and fruits, these flowers and candles. They wouldn't have to mention the values at stake, because they would think them too evident and obvious. Of course we want to provide for our families' health and sustain life, of course we want to ensure that each enjoys himself or herself, of course we want it to be pleasant and fun, and so on. Only the philosopher wants to highlight what is obvious because the neglect of the obvious leads to the distortions that come from the reductionist view that shoppers are expressing desires and satisfying preferences. While this might also be true, it does not comprehend the full reality of what is going on. For that we have to refer to the values which give the sense, the point of it all.

Values are abstract, while goods are concrete. The values tell us why exactly the goods we pursue are indeed good, and worth pursuing. Their goodness does not depend on our happening to want them: we want them because of their real goodness, the nutritious quality of the joint of beef, its flavour as something special, as a tribute to the guests we will receive and feed with it. That real goodness of the goods we work for makes them appear worth pursuing because of how they fit into our overall practical projects, such as our commitment to friendship and partnership, to family and community, to our business and work colleagues and to the projects that arise in these contexts.

There are two kinds of values. There is the kind of value that enables us to speak about what is worthwhile in the things we pursue and try to do. And there is another kind of value that enables us to speak about the kinds of standards that should apply to the way in which we act, and the manner in which we go about pursuing our goals. A simple example should help clarify the distinction. Friendship names a value that is at stake in our relationships with our friends. Every friend is distinctive, no two are alike, and each friend brings out something different in each of us. The friends are particular people; the time we spend with them and the things we do together are just as particular and specific: with one I enjoy philosophical argument, with another a visit to the concert hall, with a third a meal together with her family. And yet, despite the distinctiveness of each person and each relationship, and despite the particularities of activities and time and places, we can recognise something common to them all. This we name as the value of friendship. The friend is concrete and specific, as are our common activities and time together, but the value is abstract. It applies to all our friends and joint undertakings, and helps us to identify what it is about those people and our common activities that attracts us and explains why we find it worthwhile. Someone without friends and the experience of friendly relationships will find it difficult to understand what is meant by saying that friendship is the value that makes sense of these experiences. The value is shorthand for an explanation, which, however, cannot be given where the basic experience is lacking. This is one kind of value, naming the point of many of our activities. Another example is health, as the value is at stake in our visit to the doctor, the attempt to lead a healthier lifestyle, and the consumption of prescribed medicine, as much as in the whole apparatus of hospitals and medical schools. Values express the point of our activities, identifying the reason why they are worthwhile.

The other kind of value is related to the activities themselves as to the form they take. Friendship requires loyalty to our friends: that we will stand by them, defend them against slander, and refuse to be complicit in making fun of them at their expense. Friendship also requires fidelity: a commitment to the relationship, that we make the effort to keep in touch and communicate as appropriate. Generosity, consideration and sensitivity are also qualities which we might wish to have in our dealings with our friends. These values of loyalty, commitment, generosity characterise the quality of our actions with and towards our friends. They set standards to which we aspire and according to which our actions can be evaluated. Values in this second sense are generalised to give us standards that we apply across the board, including in our social and political context: values of justice, equality, freedom and respect.

Imagine you are invited to a dinner party but you don't know the hosts very well. It is up to you to enter into the party mood and make an effort to meet people and enjoy their company. You do your best but then find that you are not at ease. Suppose you become aware that the food and drink provided were the product of exploitative relationships, then the pleasure of their consumption would be compromised. And suppose you notice that the host treats the catering staff unfairly, and that the women in the company are made the butt of sexist remarks, or that the conversation veers towards endorsing racist ideology, then, as we say, 'the good would have gone out of it'. The goods of the dinner party would be lost or at least severely jeopardised in these circumstances. The harm done is of various kinds, which we can distinguish, and to prevent such harms we can also formulate standards that we would invoke in criticising disruptive behaviour.

We know the difference between being a guest at a dinner party and being a member of the catering staff. The latter is not invited to sit down at the table with the guests, so to that extent there is inequality in the treatment of the various persons present. We could say that there is discrimination in their treatment, but it is not arbitrary discrimination. There are good reasons for the difference, and none of the participants will be shocked by it. That this particular inequality in treatment is unobjectionable does not imply that any treatment is permissible. There is a basic decency in treatment which is due to every person, expressing a respect to which they are entitled. We are more readily able to recognise when the behaviour or speech is inappropriate than we are able to say precisely why certain action is wrong and what exactly is due.

The good is pursued and achieved in action, and the good of persons is also pursued through cooperation, action together. The manner in which actions are performed and how their objects are achieved are relevant to the pursuit of the good, so that when the values at stake are articulated, they can include not only the intelligibility of the goods (as life, health, nutrition make sense of a plate of food) but also the manner of the action. In that case, terms such as justice, liberty, equality, tolerance, respect and dignity can name qualities that we want to find realised in persons, actions and situations in which goods are pursued. Let us call them qualitative values. To the extent that they qualify the manner of our actions they are values that make sense of our pursuit of the good. All the things we want to achieve and realise in the dinner party – nutrition, friendship, play, aesthetic experience – we want to achieve under certain conditions, too many to elucidate, but any one of which, if absent, could destroy the mood of the occasion – take the good out of it. That people be treated with respect, that the dignity of each one and of the occasion be recognised, that tolerance be shown towards the differences and idiosyncrasies of the participants, that equality be insofar realised that no one feels unfairly treated, that each one be allowed the space to be themselves at the party and that the whole set of relationships sustaining the occasion be just, from the sourcing of the food and drink to the treatment of suppliers and employees. This way of considering these qualitative values maintains the focus on the concrete goods, which are pursued in action. The additional values qualify how the goods are pursued.

Another way of putting this is to highlight the abstraction involved in speaking about pursuing justice or liberty or equality. These are useful abstractions and conveniently summarise long lists of concrete goods and the manner of their attainment. The striking employees of a firm may say they want justice: what they are seeking is a fair wage or more humane working conditions. The litigant seeks justice, meaning she wants a judgement that vindicates her case always with a particular content: a barring order against an abusive partner, an enforcement of paternity payments or a remedy against a neglectful landlord. And similarly when we speak of equality we are focusing either on some outcome to be equalised or some access to resources or opportunities. Equality as such is never simply the goal of our pursuit.

Values of both kinds are in play in everything we do. In pursuing our interests through politics, in attempting to make a deal in business, we are engaging in activities that are aimed at goals in which some values are at stake, and in our actions we are always conforming to some standards appropriate to characteristic values. A key word in this sentence is 'some': some values, some standards. The reality and complexity of human affairs are such that there is a vast range of values of both kinds that can be in play in those affairs.

This is an initial clarification of basic terms. The point of the clarification is not intended as laying down rules to regulate how these terms are to be used – that would be a futile exercise. And yet the fluidity with which these terms are used in practice can be confusing, and can lead to misunderstanding between different speakers and authors, unless we have available to us some means of clarifying what is at stake. The distinctions between concrete good and value, and between the two senses of value as the abstract intelligibility of goods and the qualitative manner of action are proposed as tools to facilitate such clarification. The term 'common good' can be used to range over many instances of the objectives of action and cooperation, and not exclusively to refer to concrete goods. It is also meaningful to speak of values as common goods. In such a case, however, the challenge for an interpreter is to identify how the value that is the supposed common good of the cooperation translates into actual concrete goods, either as the goals of action, or as the desired manner in which the actions are performed.

To identify something as a common good of cooperation between certain people and to affirm that what they pursue is truly worthwhile, for instance a new school for their children in an area in which there is insufficient provision, does not imply that everyone ought to pursue this good. There is no obligation to pursue every good – such an obligation would make no sense. People choose between options that are good and attractive, as we see every year as students select their preferences for study at university via the CAO and UCAS. One student opts for medicine in preference to architecture, while another opts for science teaching in preference to veterinary science. The choices are made between possible courses at third level, which could lead to the relevant qualification as an entry to a profession. All have something good going for them, and each programme is championed by its faculty members and college. But it would be madness to think that all these goods are obligatory. It is a sufficient challenge to pursue one. What can be formulated as an obligation in relation to the goods is that each be respected and none disparaged. The student who decides against architecture ought not to disparage this profession and field of study or the people who choose it. And another negative obligation could specify that goods not be destroyed or damaged or violated. It is easier to see how obligations might be formulated in relation to the qualitative values identified above and also to recognise that the duties which are formulated negatively are more easily applied than those which are formulated positively. Justice, equality, respect, toleration and loyalty name standards that we expect to apply to the way in which we act in pursuit of the goods which attract us. The vast literature in ethics reflects the difficulties in formulating the requirements these standards impose on us, but in general we can say that it is easier to identify cases of injustice, or disrespect, or disloyalty, or inequality than to specify what exactly doing justice or showing respect requires of us. This is often spoken of as the difference between perfect duties and imperfect duties. 'Do not murder' imposes a clear duty, and while there may be difficult cases, it is usually clear what that requires of us. By contrast, 'love your neighbour as yourself' also imposes a duty, but it is not easy to say what exactly that requires of us. Similarly, the injunction to respect and care for common goods might not suggest to us exactly what we should do, but at least it would entail that we not harm or destroy or disparage our common goods.

Chapter Three
Is the Common Good Catholic?

The concept of the common good is such a central part of Catholic social thought (CST) that common good is seen by many as exclusive to Catholics. For centuries other Christians have been reluctant to use the language of the common good because it seemed to lack biblical foundations. Those for whom the task of the Church or Churches was the preaching of the gospel were suspicious of any teachings that were not directly linked to the Word of God. And Jesus in the gospels or Paul in his letters did not use the term. Can philosophical ideas be integrated with the message of the Bible?

The language of common goods was imported into theology from Greek philosophy and particularly but not exclusively from Aristotle. The philosophical resources were useful for Christian thinkers who wanted to understand the nature and role of church, and of authority, and to clarify the relationship between the Christian community and the civil and political communities in which it was situated. This was a complex and turbulent history that saw Christians divided between those who welcomed and celebrated the partnership of the Church with the Roman Empire and those who always pointed to the transcendent mission of the Church, which no political power could deliver. The Reformation did not resolve this tension but made it worse, as states and peoples were labelled with the religious affiliation of their rulers. Only now since the late twentieth century is the Catholic Church really freeing itself from the baggage of association with political power, and debates about whether the Vatican should continue to exploit the notion of being a state among other states, and whether the Church should continue to send ordained bishops as ambassadors to the governments of other states reflect the ongoing tension.

The language of the common good and of common goods was useful for dealing with such issues, and can continue to be a resource for those thinking their way through the complex questions. For instance, if religion and politics are about common goods, is the same common good pursued by the Church and by the state? Should the state be an instrument for the pursuit of the common good as envisaged by the Church? Still, the original objection to this language as non-biblical, a foreign import, remains a question to be answered, not least because Catholic believers are now much more reliant on the New Testament scriptures to nourish their faith. And in fact many non-Catholic Christian scholars are now adopting the language of common goods and making it their own. This is because of the suitability of the language of the common good for communicating the shared Christian concern that the gospel should impact on social reality.

Actually, philosophical tools can be a great help in reading scripture, in seeing how seemingly contradictory texts might be reconciled with one another, or how a reader might choose between alternative interpretations. For instance, Jesus says to the rich young man who asked about the commandments he should follow, 'Go, sell what you have, and give to the poor, and you will have treasure in heaven; and come, follow me!' (Mk 10:21) How should we take this? Is this another commandment like the traditional ones mentioned: do not kill; do not bear false witness? Is this intended as a commandment meant for everyone, or only for the followers of Jesus, or just for this one young man? Some of the disciples of St Francis of Assisi caused a lot of trouble in the Church by insisting that it applied to all Christians, and so they challenged the wealth of individual prelates and the right of the Church itself to own property. (This dispute forms the background to the Umberto Eco novel and subsequent film, *The Name of the Rose*.)

Applying a little logic can help us see what Jesus must have meant. A commandment to do something presupposes that the required action can be done. But it is not possible for everyone to sell what they own; if everyone is a seller then no one is a buyer, so nothing is sold, and no money is given to the poor. Perhaps it applies only to followers of the Lord? The same objection can be made if the society is mostly Christian: the market is saturated with all the goods being sold, and the few buyers around can dictate prices. Nothing much is made for the poor, and the Christians end up totally dependent on the few with all the wealth. Actually, the Christian community had to go through this experience in history to see what Jesus meant: the Acts of the Apostles record how the early community of Christians in Jerusalem did just what Jesus had commanded: they sold everything and pooled the resources to share among the community (Acts 2:44–5; 4:32–7). Deacons had to be appointed to manage the distribution fairly and avoid conflict between the groups (Acts 6:1–3). They believed that they would not have to wait long for the return of the Risen Lord and the end of time. Eventually they had consumed all their resources – persecutions made the situation worse – and St Paul had to beg on their behalf and collect money in Corinth and elsewhere among Near Eastern Christian communities to bring back to Jerusalem (2 Cor 8:4; 9:1–15). Jesus' commandment can be meaningful if it is meant for this individual young man, and perhaps others also, who like him wonder how much more they might offer the Lord. So the Church has learnt to distinguish between commandments intended for all humans and those intended for all believers, and to recognise a special category known as the Evangelical Counsels. These distinctions are not explicit in the biblical text, but the act of distinguishing helps clarify what is meant by making explicit what is already implied.

This is the kind of answer St Thomas Aquinas would give to the accusation that his use of Greek categories in the interpretation of the Christian gospel distorts the message. He would point to the way in which the philosophical distinctions and categories enable us to excavate their full meaning from the often terse and cryptic words of Jesus and of the scriptures. This applies also to the language of goods and common goods when brought to the understanding of the biblical message.

Let us look again at the story of the rich young man. Jesus reacted to his initial address, 'good teacher', by responding curtly: 'Why do you call me good? No one is good but God alone!' The philosophical distinction between goodness itself and goodness by participation is useful for interpreting the words of Jesus, as well as the passages about creation from the Book of Genesis (Mk 10:17–22). No one? Does Jesus really want to deny his own goodness? Does he want to deny the goodness of the young man, who has kept all these commandments from his youth? Does he want to deny the message of the creation story from the Book of Genesis that God saw all that he had made, that it was good, and indeed it was very good? (Gn 1:31) So what could Jesus mean by asserting so bluntly that 'no one is good but God alone'?

With Aquinas, using a little philosophy, we can say that God is goodness itself, and that everything which is not God, but which is good according to its kind, has its goodness *from* God. In the sense that only God is good in himself, then it is true to say that nothing else is good in itself, but that whatever goodness things have they have from goodness itself. Participation is the notion used to explain this relation of having goodness in a limited measure from an unlimited source of goodness. The convenient example to illustrate participation is to point to the light of the moon which is reflected sunlight. In terms of energy we are aware now how much our sources of energy on earth are from the sun. Fossil fuels are derived from dead organisms that once lived by transferring the energy of the sun's light into vegetative matter. This idea of participation is used also to make sense of creation, and the relationship of creature to the creator.

But what about Jesus himself? If we acknowledge him as the Son of God, God made man, the Word made flesh, doesn't that mean that he must be equal in dignity to the Father? This only heightens the urgency of the question posed: how could Jesus deny the goodness of himself or mean that he only has the participated goodness which belongs to creatures? It is useful to look at what Jesus says elsewhere about his relationship with the Father to deal with this. Even in this relationship, as it is made known to us through the Gospel of St John, Jesus claims that all that he has is from the Father (Jn 15:15; 16:15), yet this doesn't seem to be a relationship of dependence, or subjugation, or hierarchy in the usual human sense, because he also claims identity with the Father: 'I and the Father are one' (Jn 10:30). Given this rich set of claims, it is unlikely that with his question to the young man Jesus wished to deny the goodness of himself or to claim only the goodness of creatures. More likely, instead, that his question was a challenge to the young man to move beyond the respectful address 'good teacher', which might express no more than good manners or even flattery, and to make a commitment, one that could sustain the kind of renunciation of his wealth to which Jesus called him.

The good is the object of desire, and insofar as beings are drawn towards the same good it is said to be their common good on condition that its achievement would complete or perfect them. Conifer trees, such as fir and spruce, crowded together in a monoculture plantation grow tall and straight, because each is drawn towards the sunlight, its source of energy for growth and flourishing. The sunlight is their common good, as is their flourishing, and this remains true even if, as is the case, they compete with one another for the share of sunlight. By analogy with the sunlight, God as goodness itself is the common good of all that is, and of all that strives for its own fulfilment. The medieval theologians were able to make such claims without fearing the ridicule of natural scientists. But the absence of appreciation for such a perspective is at the heart of the environmental crisis whereby, as Pope Francis remarks in his letter *Laudato Si'* (Praise Be to You), humans have damaged their common home. And so he recalls his readers to a respect for the goodness in everything that is. This is an appeal for a vision of the good, not an imposition of duties or norms. It is the appreciation of the good at stake which will ensure that people taking advantage of the earth and its resources will respect proper limits and will be careful not to destroy what is there for everyone to enjoy.

My discussion above of the situation of the early Christian community in Jerusalem may perhaps appear as one-sided. Yes, they were misled by their assumption that the end would soon come and that the Lord would return and bring to an end familiar worldly existence. But that cannot be the whole story. The brief descriptions given in the early chapters of the Acts of the Apostles point to very wonderful and beautiful features of a common life, rooted in common prayer, the ritual 'breaking of the bread' which we now know as the Eucharist, the sharing of goods, care for the vulnerable and the needy, and the witness to their neighbours of the depth of their commitment to the common faith. These accounts have survived, not as a testimony to the illusion or shared misapprehension about the end of time, but as testimony to the conviction that the call of Jesus demanded a radically new form of life not only for individuals but for communities and for human society in general. They strove to find that newness of life in practices, which in one respect turned out to be unsustainable but nonetheless reflected commitment to love, to self-giving, to compassion and to sharing. Then as now, these practices are countercultural. To speak about them it helps to use the terms from Greek philosophy that are not directly in the text, but which help us make sense of the texts. As every society is united by having common goods so this particular Christian society is marked off from its surrounding cultural environment by its distinctive goods in common. Those goods do not include wealth in the material sense, since they pool their resources not to increase or maximise them but to share them among the needy. Their goods do not include power in the military or political sense, as is evident from the other stories in the context. Neither is there a pursuit of status or pre-eminence or honour, even though the text reports that they were much admired, but the practice of daily prayer suggests their lifestyle was focused on the honour and praise of God. What then is the common good which united the early Church in Jerusalem? It must be at the level of their shared meaning, the convictions and values that ground their commitment to the common life. Much of their activity, such as their prayer and their preaching, was focused on renewing and expanding that central good in their lives, for which they had various metaphors and images.

The Kingdom of God proclaimed by Jesus was fundamental to their aspirations. To be subject to the rule of God assuring justice and the fulfilment of the prophets' dreams of a world of peace, plenty and inclusion was what they hoped for. These goods, the objects of their desire and longing, were their common goods. Jesus declared himself brother and friend to his followers. He not only said but accepted the consequences that love of one's friends could cost one's life. So, the community of his followers were united by this one good – having a friend in common – and being committed to friendship on the same terms as Jesus.

Jesus had explained the purpose of his life and death, 'that they may have life, and have it abundantly' (Jn 10:10). Abundant life, the fullness of life, that is the good they pursue in common, the common good which gives the point and *raison d'etre* of the community of believers. But what does it mean?

Other verses explain that eternal life is to know God, and his anointed one, Jesus (Jn 17:3). Much can be made of that notion of 'knowing' in biblical terms. It refers to a deep personal unity.

And that unity is clarified further when Jesus speaks of himself as the bread of life, offering himself as nourishment for a fuller, more abundant life (Jn 6). But still we might wonder what he means by life and being fully alive.

I suggest that we reflect on the things that make Jesus really angry as a way of finding out what matters to him. If, as he says, his life has this one purpose, to enable his people to have a full life, then perhaps he will be angered by those things that prevent him achieving his purpose, the things that block people from having a full life. What causes him to be angry will be a good indicator of what he really cares about.

The scene that immediately springs to mind is the cleansing of the temple. Jesus accuses the temple merchants of turning the house of God into a den of thieves (Jn 2:13). A space in which people ought to be free to worship and bask in the presence of God has become instead a space in which they are made to pay for the privilege which should be their entitlement. This is the most explicit mention of his anger, but there are many other gospel scenes in which we can see him angry: at the hypocrisy of religious authorities whom he calls whited sepulchres and accuses of burdening people with rules and duties while refusing to help them. Other similar scenes show him angry at the religious leaders whose priorities are distorted, because they place the observance of Sabbath rules ahead of the care of people in need. The suffering, the blind and lame and possessed get Jesus' sympathy, and he is angry at those who could help but who refuse to do so, yet object to him helping because of some rule regarding Sabbath observance; when economic interests are at stake exceptions can be made – watering one's ox or ass – but not for suffering humanity. We can hear his anger behind those words. Is there anger behind the answers he gives to those who accuse him and his disciples of not fasting, or violating the Sabbath, or who object to him associating with 'sinners'? His determination is firm and unshakeable that he sides with the excluded and the needy: as physician he goes to the sick, as shepherd he seeks out the lost, as God's Anointed he goes to those who need him (Lk 19:10).

A full life would be marked by health and bodily well-being, nourished as required, yet it would be more than contented survival. It would have to mean inclusion in a community, being valued on a basis of equal dignity and entitled to participate in the best that the community has to offer. Our images above of the group of friends enjoying a joke, or a family assembled for a celebratory meal, give us some indication of what a full, flourishing life might be. This full life is the common good of everyone, and the aim of the mission that Jesus shares with his disciples. It is not easy to describe it, and every attempt must fail to some degree, because it seems to reduce a very rich and broad concept to a limited experience. This is the difficulty with our image of the entertaining story shared with friends. What we are talking about is always more than we can describe, no matter how sophisticated our language and our experience. St Paul ran into this difficulty as he found the limitations of both Greek wisdom and Hebrew theology in trying to communicate the message of the gospel. He had to rephrase the words of the prophet Isaiah to make the point: 'What no eye has seen, nor ear heard, nor the heart of man conceived, what God has prepared for those who love him' (1 Cor 2:9 referring to Is 64:4). Paul has to reach beyond what appears to Greek minds as foolishness and what seems scandalous to Jews, in order to communicate his message. In the Letter to the Ephesians in the context of a prayer of praise of God we read that the Christian disciple can be empowered to accomplish abundantly more than can be imagined (Eph 3:20). We may not be able to define justice exactly, but we certainly recognise injustice when we see it. Similarly, while we may not be able to describe the abundance of life, we can recognise its absence or denial in suffering humanity.

The reference to Paul and his struggle to find the words to communicate his message reminds us that the question addressed above about the importation of Greek philosophy into the gospel message being a distortion is a complex one. Because already in the first century proclamation of the good news Paul was drawing on Greek thought and popular philosophy to make the case for his message. In the Letter to the Philippians, Paul borrows the Stoic ideas that life as a whole has a goal, and that there is an ideal community transcending the actual failing communities in history.

For the Christian life's goal is to be a participant in an ideal community, and Jesus is the model for all who strive for this goal. Paul writes 'our commonwealth is in heaven, and from it we await a Saviour, the Lord Jesus Christ, who will change our lowly body to be like his glorious body, by the power which enables him even to subject all things to himself' (Phil 3:20–21). The Greek word that is translated in the *Revised Standard Version* as 'commonwealth' is *to politeuma* which has at its root the idea of *polis*, or city, political society. Sometimes it is translated as 'citizenship' giving 'our citizenship is in heaven'.

Paul's polemic against philosophy in 1 Corinthians might give the impression that he rejected all philosophy. The situation seems to be a little more complicated than that. Not all philosophers were the same. There were the professionals, like the Sophists of the Socratic Dialogues, who earned their living from teaching and practising the skills of debate. On the other hand, there were popularising philosophers who wandered about and attracted audiences to their talks, for which they relied on collections of ideas from various classical authors, without needing to care for attribution or representation. A standard element of their repertoire was the polemic against the professional philosophers, whose teaching provided little or no help for the living of life, and which was expensive to boot. Paul was one such itinerant popular teacher and the speech recorded for us in Acts 17:22–31, up to the point where he introduces the reference to resurrection, is typical of the popular philosophers' style with quotations from and references to a range of thinkers. In his rejection of what we might call professional philosophy, Paul is just like the popular philosophers of his day. But he changes popular teachings, retaining their form and giving them new content. He reworks the traditional concepts of *oikos* (household), *polis* (polity or city) and *basileia* (kingdom).

These are the conventional philosophical terms for speaking about political reality, even after the forms in which they originated had ceased to exist. Still, with the memory of how the Greek city state functioned with its assembly of citizens, the language was available for Paul to give new meaning to *ekklesia* (the assembly) now referring not to the gathering of citizens of Rome, or of Athens, but to the citizens of a new *polis*, gathered in the houses of the Roman believers (Rm 16:5). This Greek word, originally purely political in meaning, has through its adoption by Paul and its usage through the centuries become the Latin term for Church, *ecclesia*, and survives in the English word ecclesiastic, and cognate terms.

The Letter to the Ephesians is Pauline in tone and content – even if it may not have been written by Paul. But it relies on the familiar Greek political terms to explain to the Gentile converts their membership as believers in the community of the Church. 'So then you are no longer strangers and sojourners but you are fellow citizens with the saints and members of the household of God' (Eph 2:19). The theme of unity in the Body of Christ is important in this letter and the implied equality of all within the community, in which Gentiles or latecomers are on equal terms with Jewish converts, resonates elsewhere in Paul's writings (Gal 3:28).

The evidence from St Paul's writings is that Greek philosophical ideas were spontaneously integrated in the self-understanding of the preachers of the gospel and the leaders of communities already in the founding period of the Christian Church. This language and these concepts were drawn upon and modified to present and explain a new reality. When Saints Albert and Thomas in the medieval period adopted Greek philosophical terms such as that of the common good to explain the communal and political dimensions of Christian discipleship, they were doing nothing different from what St Paul in the first century had done. The notion of common good is indeed a key element of Catholic social thought, but it is not an exclusive Catholic possession, so to speak, since it speaks of a basic human reality on which the gospel is built. And as an element of the tradition it is offered to everyone as a resource for their own understanding of their experience.

Chapter Four
Common Goods in Catholic Social Thought

As we saw in the previous chapter, St Paul teaches Christians that 'our commonwealth is in heaven', that we are citizens of a new city, and that our ultimate goal is the salvation offered to us by Christ. For centuries Christians asked about their common good and would first have answered in terms of the community of the saved united in the Resurrection with Christ their head. This emphasis remains in the statement that the goal of development as of all our striving is the 'integral development of every person and of the whole person'. But now, since Pope John XXIII and the Second Vatican Council, the meaning of the common good is given not primarily as the ultimate goal of integral fulfilment, but as the 'sum total of social conditions which allow people, either as groups or as individuals, to reach their fulfilment more fully and more easily' (*Compendium* 164 quoting G&S 26). The full set of conditions that would enable persons and groups to achieve their fulfilment is what the Council sees as the common project of humankind. This extends across the full range of human activities and human aspirations. Human ingenuity is constantly creating new possibilities and so new conditions, coming up with new fields of endeavour, new areas of scientific exploration and new possibilities of medical and surgical intervention and care. The common good in this sense of the complete set of conditions for human flourishing would include the economic, social, cultural, legal, political, international and global.

The *Compendium of the Social Doctrine of the Church* published by the Pontifical Council for Justice and Peace lists the common good among the four permanent principles of Catholic Social Doctrine.[1] The other principles are the dignity of the human person, solidarity and subsidiarity. The *Compendium* first treats the common good and insists that its transcendent dimension not be overlooked: God is the ultimate end and Supreme Good of his creatures. The two dimensions of ultimate end and the conditions for its realisation should not be separated (*Compendium*, 170).

Evangelisation is the proclamation of this message in its fullness. This was the point of the apostolic exhortation *Evangelii Nuntiandi* 'Evangelisation in the Modern World' (1975), published by Pope Paul VI as a response to a Synod of Bishops on the topic of evangelisation. This document came out just as I was beginning the study of theology in preparation for ordination. It made a big impact on me, and has inspired both my priesthood and my work in philosophy because the Pope sets a philosophical task in calling for a radical critique of patterns of thought, and cultural values, which confine people within a limited vision of what might be possible for them. Particularly striking is his insistence that evangelisation calls for conversion not only of individuals but of collective consciences.

---

1   Published Rome: Libreria Editrice Vaticana, 2004, p. 91.

There is a real sense of urgency in the exhortation, and the tragedy is that the same urgency is still relevant today. I was inspired by Pope Paul's anger at the forces that oppress people and deprive them of their dignity, their liberty, and their opportunities for a fuller life. Just like Jesus, the promise of life in abundance has its shadow in the anger at what threatens and kills that life. Paul VI saw evangelisation as including activity designed to liberate people from everything that deprives them of life: 'Peoples struggle to overcome everything which condemns them to remain on the margin of life: famine, chronic disease, illiteracy, poverty, injustices in international relations and especially in commercial exchanges, situations of economic and cultural neo-colonialism sometimes as cruel as the old political colonialism' (*EN*, 30). Here is the shadow side of the fullness of life, enumerated by the Pope in his listing of injustice, oppression, dependency, famine, disease, ignorance and poverty. The work of evangelisation entails a proclamation, but also an engagement in practical affairs to ensure that the liberation is achieved (*EN*, 30). 'Christ proclaims salvation, this great gift of God which is liberation from everything that oppresses humanity' (*EN*, 9). Can the Pope be so clear in his formulations unless he has a deep sense of hurt and also anger in his heart at what deprives people of their humanity? And can he be unaware of what is involved in assisting in liberation? It cannot be done without social and political action. But his language acknowledges this in recognising the focus of evangelisation is not simply an invitation to individuals to accept Christ and be converted to His way. The message of the gospel is also addressed to whole cultures and communities, to what the language of the exhortation calls collective consciences: 'The Church evangelises when she seeks to convert both the personal and collective consciences of people, the activities in which they engage, and the lives and concrete milieu which are theirs' (*EN*, 18). Elsewhere in the exhortation you can see that the Pope, reflecting the discussions of the bishops at the synod, is perfectly aware of structural and systemic issues when he writes of new forms of colonialism, of patterns of economic relations which systemically impoverish some people, and of models of international relations that institutionalise injustice.

A few years earlier, in 1967, Pope Paul VI had published an important encyclical letter, *Populorum Progressio*, 'On the Development of Peoples'. Coming within a couple of years of the Second Vatican Council, it takes up the tradition of Catholic social thought and communicates it in the context of the focus on development, in the United Nations Decade for Development. There is much wise reflection on what constitutes development, and what the false or distorted images of development might look like: *having*, not *being*, consumerism, reductionism. Against these limited visions of the fullness of life, the Pope explores what is meant by the common good, and answers the question in terms of the integral fulfilment of every person and of the whole person. One can see immediately the consistency between Paul VI writing in 1967 and Paul VI writing in 1975: in both there is the recognition of the fullness of life as central to the message of the gospel, the concern to elaborate what that entails, and at the same time to spell out the shadow side, the blocks to people achieving their integral fulfilment, and the false images which can divert people away from the path to true development. The big difference between the documents, however, is not really in what is said, but the manner in which it is said. Where the 1967 encyclical is calm and reflective, the 1975 exhortation is engaged and spirited. The analysis of development in the encyclical is profound, and measured, but the proclamation of liberation in the exhortation is full of energy and emotion. It barely conceals the anger felt at all that deprives people of life that oppresses them and holds them in such situations of powerlessness. And the hope offered to those oppressed and impoverished is a lifeline thrown in the reminder of Christ's offer of deliverance and the Church's commitment to assist in that liberation, and see it to completion.

The 1967 encyclical on development has become one of the milestones in the century of Catholic social thought, meriting commemorative letters marking twenty and forty years after its publication. In 1987 Pope John Paul II published his encyclical letter *Sollicitudo Rei Socialis*, 'On Social Concern', to mark its twentieth anniversary. He makes solidarity a special theme. Solidarity, he writes, 'is not a feeling of vague compassion or shallow distress at the misfortunes of so many people, both near and far. On the contrary, it is a firm and persevering determination to commit oneself to the common good; that is to say to the good of all and of each individual, because we are all really responsible for all' (*SRS*, 38). Like his predecessor, Pope John Paul is clear about the need on the part of the Church and all Christians for a firm commitment to changing the circumstances that deprive people of their humanity and deny them the prospect of a decent life. Engagement, commitment, action, not just proclamation, but assistance and collaboration until the liberation is complete (*EN*, 30). Radical change requires firm commitment and collaboration.

Pope Benedict XVI in 2009 marked the fortieth anniversary of Paul's development encyclical with his own letter, *Caritas in Veritate*, 'Love in Truth'. Here there is no reduction in urgency, but a reinforcement of the view that the shadow side involves structures and systems that need to be confronted and changed. 'Paul VI understood development to indicate the goal of rescuing peoples from hunger, deprivation, endemic diseases and illiteracy' (*CV*, 21). All the dehumanising factors are listed, but also the need for a corrective which brings about a different form of economy in which people are not just a factor of production, a different society marked by equality, and a different politics oriented to freedom and peace.

This is just a brief survey of some of the rich heritage of Catholic social thought, and specifically in a series of three letters and an exhortation that constitute a single strand in the tradition. But it helps us to fill out what we might understand Jesus to mean when he promises his people the fullness of life, and when he shows his anger at the things depriving his people of that very life. It maps out for us the sources of inspiration for social action in service of the Church and God's people.

Jesus gets angry at the wrongdoing of the people in the temple who are abusing it and its purpose. Similarly, our popes point with anger to all those things that deny people their development or fulfilment and the social, economic and political conditions which entrap them and deny them a human existence. It is also possible for us to identify the many forms of wrongdoing: there are people who actively cause these problems, others who are complicit, and still others who benefit without appreciating the extent of their collusion in harming others. Hence, Pope Paul VI underlined the agenda of evangelisation to change, to convert, the judgements, values and activities of those associated in any way with the oppression of their fellow humans: 'The Church evangelises when she seeks to convert both the personal and collective consciences of people, the activities in which they engage, and the lives and concrete milieu which are theirs' (*EN*, 18).

Conversion brings about a change not only in what one does but in what one loves. The change is towards solidarity, a firm commitment to the common good, also formulated as the integral fulfilment of every person and of the whole person. We might wonder at the formulation of obligations to serve the common good. If it is loved, why does it need to be commanded? Many wonder at the point of commanding love: 'love God and love your neighbour as yourself'. If it needs to be commanded, can it be love? And anything less than love would be pointless, as for instance a performance for appearances sake. But for someone who is in love, who is gripped by love and desires to love, such a person experiences the call to love as a commandment, a demand, made to him by the reality and the presence of the beloved.

Similarly, for those committed to the common good of their communities. Each one will have found his or her own way to the realisation of what is required of them: from the guidance of another who has opened their eyes to what is possible, from the attractiveness of a model such as Pope Francis who provides an example that might be imitated, or possibly from the experience of exposure to injustice and oppression which motivates a search for what ought to be instead of what has been. Those drawn to promotion and service of the common goods of their communities can speak of a command to love and serve, and like Jesus, and the Popes, they can speak out against those violations which deny persons and their communities their proper fulfilment.

The obligation to serve the common good can be formulated in both negative and positive norms. The negative ones are more urgent, since they require people to stop the wrong they are doing, and the specific wrong can be named. The positive norms are more general and therefore vague, since while they require promotion and pursuit of goods they do not specify exactly how this should be done. A lot is left to the discretion of each person who is drawn according to circumstances and capacities as well as opportunities to one or other good, to one or other form of service. As mentioned above, we can find inspiration in the words of Jesus and the popes, in particular when they discuss the suffering of humanity. These inspirational words could attract people to a commitment to the common good out of a sense of solidarity and compassion.

Following him through death to resurrection, the disciples of Jesus are to enjoy the vision of God in the company of all the saints. What exactly will this be like, the fullness of life, the vision of God, knowledge of the Father? We don't know, we cannot know, beyond the assurance that it will exceed our wildest dreams (1 Cor 2:9). Small wonder then that the reflections of Christian writers have tended to concentrate on the shadow side, the problems that will be solved, the injustices that will be resolved, the poverty and deprivation that will be overcome in abundance. The images from the Hebrew scriptures also stress the dynamic of deliverance from slavery and subjection in Egypt and of return from exile in Babylon. More positively, images of banquets and abundance, and of vindication and justice are also mined from these scriptures to communicate the hope of Christians.

In announcing a common good, Christian writers have named this as the shared goal of all of God's children, to see the Lord face-to-face in heaven, to receive and enjoy salvation. St Paul reminded his bishop friend Timothy and the readers of his letters that it is God's will that all people be saved (1 Tm 2:4). That is the destiny offered to all men, women and children, and which they are invited to accept in freedom. The Second Vatican Council in its *Lumen Gentium*, 'Dogmatic Constitution on the Church', repeated this promise and situated the mission of the Church in this context: to communicate the universal call of all to holiness, and to assist in providing the resources that Jesus makes available to his pilgrim people on their way to this destiny. The twentieth-century reformulation of the same first-century message of Paul contains the same elements: it is offered to all, everyone without exception, and based on a promise which requires confidence and trust in the one promising rather than detailed comprehension of what is promised.

In Christian tradition the supreme common good was identified as God, and the vision of God, the ultimate goal of Christian striving and the fullness of life prepared by the Creator for his creatures. It is noticeable, however, that in the twentieth century, beginning with Pope John XXIII's encyclical letter *Mater et Magistra*, 'Mother and Teacher' (1961), the common good came to be used in speaking not of the ultimate goal of human striving, but of the conditions and resources that would facilitate the achievement of that purpose. This is not contradictory, since it is generally accepted that whoever wills the end wills the means, and so the common good as the goal of common action must incorporate the means and conditions as well as the ultimate end. The point of the shift of emphasis became clearer in the context of the general realignment of Catholic thought in the mid-twentieth century. The Church saw the need to shift from a defensive and fearful stance over and against the secular, to a more positive engagement with the world. As the opening words of *Gaudium et Spes*, the 'Pastoral Constitution on the Church in the World of Today', put it, the Church identifies herself with and shares in 'the joy and hope, fear and anxiety of the men and women of today'. The Council wanted to address all men and women, not just faithful members of the Church, and not just believers in Christ, or in God, but all. And so, the recognition that while all of these addressees will not share the same ultimate vision, they might nonetheless be able to agree on what conditions and resources would help people achieve their vision of the good life, whatever it might turn out to be. 'The common good embraces the sum total of all those conditions of social life which enable individuals, families, and organisations to achieve complete and effective fulfilment' (GS, 74).

Published in 1966, the Pastoral Constitution draws on the earlier language of Pope John's encyclical to focus on the set of conditions for human fulfilment. Undeniably, the theme of fulfilment both for individuals and for communities is at the heart of the statement, but the focus is on conditions. Whatever vision people might have of the flourishing of persons and communities, and however these visions might differ, the notion of fulfilment or flourishing itself must point to conditions on which they might agree and for the achievement of which they could cooperate. Here we see the opening to the world of the Council: the desire to have a basis for cooperation with people of good will who might not share in the Church's ultimate convictions but still will seek human development and fulfilment.

The full set of conditions that would enable persons and groups to achieve their fulfilment is what the Council sees as the common project of humankind. This extends across the full range of human activities and human aspirations. No list, however long, would be exhaustive, but an initial listing of principal headings will help us bear in mind the complexity of the complete set of conditions for human flourishing. We will survey the economic, social, cultural, legal, political, international and global conditions in the following paragraphs, and examine some of them in more depth in later chapters.

At the international level, a fundamental condition for human well-being anywhere and everywhere is peace; not only the absence of war, but friendly relations between states. For the securing of these conditions the countries of the world have attempted to create institutions so that conflicts can be managed in time to prevent the outbreak of war. The League of Nations was an early attempt in the aftermath of the First World War (1914–18), and the United Nations followed the Second World War (1939–45). The UN might be seen to be more of a success story than the earlier League, but that success is only partial at best. While the conflagration of nuclear war has been avoided, there have been proxy wars between the superpowers, as well as local and regional armed conflicts. The present situation of global terrorism makes clear to all that no part of the world can claim to be assured of peace. Peace at the international level is an important condition but it is not easily achieved, nor is it easily maintained. The rule of law at an international level is still in the process of creation, and it is only by analogy with established state law that one can speak of international law: there is no comparable executive authority to enforce law which depends largely on the willing cooperation of states.

States vary considerably in the manner in which they manage the issues of the allocation of powers and authority and in the design of institutions for government, law-making and adjudication. That variation can be a product of historical circumstance but also of accommodation to the distinctive characters of different peoples. What is a suitable structure of government in a particular place may be a matter of dispute. A constitution and customary practices of government assign powers and responsibilities not only to office holders but also to citizens and their groupings. Conditions for human well-being at this level can be complex, and we can note how some questions, such as the desirability of an upper house, the Senate, are open to debate. Also in the current post-Brexit situation in Ireland, the involvement in joint cross-border institutions.

Whatever the form and structure of government, it will need to have structures for the making of law, the adjudication of cases, and the executive implementation of law and court decisions. In considering legal systems as conditions for the fulfilment of humans, both as individuals and as groups, it is difficult to imagine how they might successfully provide such conditions unless they incorporate what we now regard as basic human rights: the protection of the right to life, of freedom of conscience, of speech, of assembly, of religion. The guarantee of freedom from arbitrary arrest, from torture or inhumane treatment, the assurance of the inviolability of one's home and property, must also be among the basic rights secured for people. And in relevant respects there must be an exclusion of discrimination on arbitrary grounds, of race, ethnicity, religion, sexual orientation, or political affiliation. Beyond espousal of these values in law, there has to be effective implementation.

Cultural conditions should allow individuals and communities the freedom and the opportunity to express their identity, confident in their sense of self-worth. This is a complex reality, and it is not easily described. The temptation is to rely on categories that give the impression of clarity and strict boundaries. But even an initial exploration of the reality on the ground reveals a complexity that defies comprehension in sharply drawn boundary lines. Members of various communities will hardly be able to flourish unless they enjoy a sense of confidence that they are accepted for who and what they are and that their cultural identity, while being respected, will not be a block to them making progress and achieving whatever goals they set themselves in life.

On the level of the social conditions for the flourishing of individuals and groups the scope is immense. For instance, the range of sporting clubs is considerable. But sport is just one area of social interaction that provide people in families, church groups, CSOs and clubs with the occasions to meet and act together.

All the other conditions presuppose the economic. Without the production and distribution of goods and services and the access to resources they depend on, the wealth generated by them, and the credit which oils their functioning, it would not be possible to have systems of law and government, and cultural identity would have little scope for expression. This is why access to a share in the activities of wealth creation and consumption is fundamental for the enjoyment of any of the other goods which life makes available to people. The possibility of owning some property of one's own is a prerequisite for the exercise of responsibility and the enjoyment of autonomy.

Even more of a concern for CST than the usefulness of property is the status of human work. Since the first nineteenth-century engagement of Pope Leo XIII with the phenomenon of modern capitalist economic systems in *Rerum Novarum* (1891) the popes have repeated the insistence that human work not be treated just as a factor of production that has a cost, a cost which employers are constantly motivated to minimise. Workers are persons, human beings who by their willing cooperation and the application of their physical and intellectual capacities contribute to the communal projects of meeting human need and providing the cultivated, manufactured, and built environment in which human life can flourish. Culminating in the letter of Pope John Paul II explicitly devoted to the topic of work, *Laborem Exercens*, 'On Human Work' (1981), the popes have maintained a constant insistence that work and the status of the worker is at the heart of the social question. Unemployment, the lack of opportunity to work, is fundamentally undermining of the sense of dignity and self-worth of human beings, who rely on their work to provide for their families and who without the earnings that come from honest work are unable to meet their obligations. Especially those without advanced skill sets whose work is primarily physical, contributing muscle power, are vulnerable to the vagaries of job markets. Not only adequate remuneration but also appropriate working conditions belong among the conditions for human fulfilment, which the tradition names as comprising the common good in the political sense.

In summary, we can identify one key distinction in CST between the ultimate common good, God who is goodness itself, and the means and conditions which will enable individuals and groups to attain their ultimate fulfilment. These conditions can be further distinguished into familiar categories from the international to the economic; throughout, however, the focus of CST is on the human person, whether as the worker in an economy or as the subject of attention in development policy, because it is the integral fulfilment of *every* person and of the *whole* person which is the goal.

Chapter Five
Does the Economy Have a Common Good?

In the old Soviet Union a shopper went to buy a pair of shoes, and on entering the shop was surprised to find the shelves all empty. When she said to the assistant that she wanted winter walking shoes, the reply was, 'sorry, we are a bakery, here we have no bread; next door they have no shoes!' This story was typical of the humour that arose from the experience of living in a centrally controlled economy.

If the key to the market economy is that everyone pursues their own private good, and that the fostering of economic freedom is important for political freedom, doesn't it follow that there can't be any place for common goods in a free market economy in a pluralist society? When talking about common goods and especially the tradition of Catholic social thought on the common good – the one area in which people raise strong objections is the economy. The economy has nothing to do with common goods, it is alleged. It is the forum in which people compete as sellers of goods and services or as consumers at an auction outbidding one another, or as sellers and buyers haggling over prices and conditions. The economy is the arena in which some people get wealthy and others lose everything, so if there is some good in common it doesn't seem to impact on the economy. The phenomena of industrial disputes show how embattled the economic interests of the people are, in tension with one another and not in collaboration. The usual debates on the economy reflect the same lack of cohesion around common goods: nationalisation vs privatisation, deficit budgeting vs fiscal rectitude, cut income taxes to stimulate consumer spending vs cut corporate taxes to facilitate saving and investment, restrict government expenditure on welfare and healthcare and focus instead on generating sources of revenue to pay for these benefits, and so on. The questions are real and do indeed pose a serious challenge to any talk about common goods in the context of the economy. And it is not an answer to such challenges to speak of some ideal of how things ought to be, or to spell out demanding moral norms which are untenable in practice.

Karl Marx began his analysis of the economy with the observation of a simple fact: at the same time as we produce wealth, we also produce poverty. 'We' here refers to humankind, our societies, as they go about producing and distributing all that is needed to live decently. This paradoxical fact, that both wealth and poverty are products of human activity that are somehow linked, was the central phenomenon to be explained. Economic science which failed to cope with this fact was to be dismissed as ideological irrelevance, merely concealing the paradox behind a smokescreen of verbiage that protected the interests of those benefitting from the wealth creation. Marx produced some examples to illustrate his point: construction workers who build palaces for the rich are themselves obliged to live in hovels, as we can see in Qatar and other Gulf States today; textile factory workers who produce beautiful garments are themselves confined to a miserable life, as we can see in the conditions of textile workers in Bangladesh.

Are Marx's examples time-bound? Do they apply only to the mid-nineteenth century, to the early years of industrialisation? Those who find his account implausible now point to the benefits that workers gain from employment, even if it means hard work. They argue that people are better off in jobs, even dirty, demanding jobs, than to be without work and a source of earned income. No one, they say, will willingly contract into an employment, unless they expect it to bring them benefits and improve their situation. They do not deny that the situations in which people find themselves can indeed be dire, but one pathway to improvement is to take a job, and no one takes a job unless they believe it will help to make things better.

Unfortunately, this response, although plausible, does not address Marx's key point, which is that the poverty we observe is as much a product of our economic activity as is our wealth. This response refuses to enter into the paradox that our systems for the production of what we need also bring about impoverishment and dehumanisation. Perhaps we need more twenty-first century examples to identify the same fact that motivated Marx's analysis. Our examples today must be drawn from a global horizon, and not only from local and national contexts. Our economy now is global. The shirts I wear are manufactured no longer in Derry or Manchester, but in Bangladesh, or Indonesia, or Malaysia. The mobile phone I use may have a Japanese brand label, but its parts are assembled among other things from minerals mined in East Congo, where warlords finance their fighting from the sale of coltan or tantalite. My laptop is assembled in Ireland, but its parts are sourced from factories in Korea, Singapore and India. The distance may mean that I can remain ignorant of the conditions under which the work is done, but that involves turning a blind eye to news reports of the collapse of textile factories in Bangladesh, or the plight of Rwandan migrants in the Congo. The world will be entertained by the football World Cup in Qatar in 2022, but the construction workers enduring the desert heat suffer dreadful conditions to make it possible. The closure of a local plant in my neighbourhood because the work can be more cheaply sourced in Indonesia; the closure of an Irish call centre because of relocation to the Philippines, will of course warrant headlines bemoaning the loss of Irish jobs, but the uncomfortable truth behind this is that everyone is competing with others, even very distant others. We lose our jobs to people who are prepared to work for less and who are willing to accept poorer working conditions.

These twenty-first century examples highlight the continuing relevance of Marx's observation, that our wealth-producing efforts bring forth poverty as well as wealth, create ugliness as well as beauty and stupefy while generating intelligence. The production and assembly line tasks involved in the manufacture of our electronic gadgets can illustrate this last point. While the smartphone is an extremely intelligent instrument with more software built in to it than I could ever hope to exploit, the production processes with their repetitive tasks are unlikely to have fostered the intelligence and creativity of the workers on the production line. Marx's remark that workers become servants of the machine instead of the machines serving the workers is as true of our contemporary factories as of those two centuries ago. The fact remains. Of course, it is not all bad.

Machines have removed the drudgery and hardship from many tasks; production lines on which robots do the heavy lifting make for a cleaner and more comfortable workplace.

But there is a new phenomenon more evident to us today in our globalised world than in the nineteenth century, although Marx did seem to grasp something of the dynamics behind it. This is the phenomenon of growing inequality even as the wealth production of the world expands. Of course, inequality is not the same as poverty. However, the observed growing inequality in our world is that between the extremes, where the extreme at the lower end of the spectrum is very poor indeed. This is not to deny the achievement of our economic systems over the recent decades in raising millions of people out of dire poverty even as the numbers of the earth's population have been growing. The success story in some respects is impressive. In some respects, I emphasise, because it is also the case that there are other features of our economic system that are less impressive. It is a convenient remark for politicians, but nonetheless true, that, contrary to expectations, younger generations are less well off than their parents' and grandparents' generations. The exception, of course, is for those who inherit wealth. This is due to the imbalance in earning power between assets and work. Work is no longer a pathway to affluence, when work is understood as paid employment in a job.

Will President Donald Trump be able to deliver on the promise he made in his campaign for the US presidency, to repatriate jobs that had been exported to other locations with lower labour costs? The exporters had been people like himself, business people, interested in cutting costs, and wanting to generate a greater revenue for executives and shareholders. He, as president, will not be able to coerce business to follow political directives. And yet millions of voters were persuaded by him, convinced that he understood their plight as victims of dynamics that took good-paying traditional jobs away from them. Whatever their hopes and prospects for change, their actual experience is of a narrowing jobs market with diminishing security and stability. Some commentators attempt to describe this situation in positive terms, as offering opportunities to people for self-redefinition and retraining, and adaptability to changing circumstances. Those in favour of zero-hours contracts describe them in positive terms as facilitating the freedom and autonomy of people who want flexibility to choose when and for how long they will work. Undoubtedly this will be true of some, but for many for whom such contracts are all that is on offer, the work is insufficient to pay their ordinary living costs. Just as Irish workers are directly affected by plant closures due to international competition, so too many find that the only jobs available to them are low-paying and insecure.

Economists have coined a new term to describe the people who find themselves in this insecure situation, calling them 'the precariat'. Evidently this is echoing Marx's term for those who own nothing but their labour power, who have nothing to sell except their capacity to work – the proletariat. The precariat is also in this situation – the difference being that the opportunities to work are narrower, in jobs which offer remuneration often just barely sufficient to pay for subsistence, and in some cases not even that. The term 'precariat' serves to highlight the fact that the numbers affected by this kind of insecurity are significant and increasing. It is not just a special minority group that is facilitated by the availability of zero-hours contracts. More and more workers now find themselves in the precarious situation of unreliable work and insecure income.

Inequality appears in a grotesque form when the bonuses and remuneration packages for executives in firms are contrasted with the average earnings of employees in those firms, or in the economy as a whole. How can it be that the contribution of those individuals to the corporate effort can warrant such a disproportionate reward? Even the severance packages or so-called golden handshakes given to departing executives whose stewardship of their firms or banks has been less than successful leaves workers dismayed, considering their own earnings in comparison.

Economists have a term for this phenomenon: 'rent-taking'. Those who hold or control an asset that is required for the functioning of a business exploit their holding to extract a share of the revenue. It is similar to the rent which the owner of property may charge for its use. In business terms the property may be land or buildings, but it can also be licenses, patents or specialist knowledge, which the holder exploits for reward. Those who hold privileged positions in organisations, such as directors, chairmen and executives, can exploit their position to squeeze more reward from the business. This is made all the easier when the people making the decisions about rewards and bonuses are the equivalent people in organisations who stand to benefit from a culture that rewards their kind of position disproportionately. Of course, shareholders at firms' annual general meetings have the opportunity to challenge such packages, and this sometimes, but all too rarely, occurs. But shareholders have a difficult task countering arguments that the greater payments must be made because otherwise the valued leader or colleague will be headhunted by a competitor. The same argument being made in all relevant organisations ensures that the culture of privileged remuneration remains intact.

Marx's fact appears to be as real today as in his time, namely, that the way in which we go about producing what we need inevitably leads to a double effect: wealth for some and poverty or hardship for others. It seems to be a feature of our system of wealth production, and so not something to be corrected with small adjustments here or there, nor in one country going it alone. We seem caught in a system the rationality of which requires the reduction of costs, and hence the export of jobs and the deskilling of tasks. We seem caught in a system in which those who already have control of assets will accrue more, while those who have nothing to bargain with are faced with ever fewer satisfactory options.

This fact is at the heart of the challenge when referring to common goods in relation to the economy. The challenge must be faced. There is no point in rushing naïvely to embrace a solution. Centralised control of the economy is not a viable option, as evidenced by the failure of the Soviet experiment. The contrast between what central control and what the free market can do has revealed the importance of information flow within the economy, with signals about needs and demands, supplies and offers flowing in all directions by means of price. Central control cannot manage such information flow, and even contributes significant distortions (as in the anecdote from the old Soviet economy: 'we pretend to work, and they pretend to pay us!'). Some prefer to opt out – to seek a simple life relying on subsistence levels of production. Even if this is viable for some, it is not an option for the millions of people in the economic system. Yet another option is protest, as in the case of the student carrying a banner at a World Economic Forum declaring: 'Replace Capitalism with Something Nice'!

None of these options are attractive from the standpoint of concern for common goods. This standpoint leads us to ask about the reality we encounter and to find goods at stake there, and potentially goods in common. A first place to start is the phenomenon of markets.

Is it not amazing that people who might have reason to fear each other as enemies and threats can nonetheless meet in a context of mutual respect? Isn't it astonishing that anonymous strangers, in large numbers, can cooperate with each other to a high degree of reliability and honesty so as to produce benefit for so many others, also unknown? The degree of interdependence and interconnectivity can be surprising when we list the provenance of the many things we buy and use: my shirts from Indonesia, gadgets from Japan, shoes from Somalia, fruits from South America, flowers from Kenya. As well as the problems listed above, of low pay and poor working conditions, there is also this marvellous phenomenon of cooperation, which is made possible by the instrument of markets. (I'm abstracting at the moment from the impact of this activity and trade on the environment.) There can be a tendency in religious circles to emphasise community and relationships of intimacy and familiarity with the result that we can underestimate the involvement with anonymous others. We take for granted this reality of interdependence and cooperation precisely because it is not face-to-face. It is there, in the background, delivering its benefits, and not attracting attention. The human activity of trading enables strangers to come together and to enter into cooperative relationships with each other. The propensity to trade has enabled the emergence of a distinctive mindset with its characteristic openness to the stranger and the willingness to enter into a deal even with a risk of loss.

Because markets facilitate the meeting of strangers for the purpose of trading they must appear as something good. Each brings something to the trade and when a deal is done each can go away with satisfaction, having acquired something that was desired in exchange for something with which it was willing to part. The grower of tomatoes has an abundance of tomatoes; the cook with a recipe for soup hasn't enough tomatoes. A sale is to the benefit of both, gardener and cook. There are questions we can ask about the conditions for markets to function satisfactorily so that the benefits are fairly distributed; I'll expand on this later, but on first glance markets must appear as goods in common to those who cooperate in maintaining and using them.

If markets are good, where then is the source of the problems we have discussed? Is it capitalism? But what is meant by capitalism? It is a way of producing wealth based on an accumulation of surplus which is invested in the business, replacing outdated machinery, building a new plant, expanding skills base, etc. Traditional agriculture must retain a surplus from the harvest, as the seed for the following season; feudal lords of the land retained a surplus to fund their military adventures, and to sustain their costly lifestyle. In both these cases there was the generation of a surplus, but it is only in capitalism that the surplus becomes a resource for investment in the business. Capital arises from the accumulated surplus of production. In this sense of capital, then even the modern socialist or communist economies were capitalist, since they reinvested some of their surplus in society's productive enterprise.

Is capital a good thing, a common good? And is capitalism as a productive system based on the investment of accumulated surplus, a good in common? To the extent that those who cooperate in the production of wealth are enabled to produce more efficiently and to generate more to be distributed then this system would belong among their common goods. A community that relied on fishing would benefit from having the resources to freeze and/or salt their catch to have it available for times when the herring or the mackerel or the tuna are not running, or the weather is too inclement to go to sea and also to be able to store it to sell in markets.

If it is possible for us to recognise the positive benefits of markets, and of capital, as useful instruments in the economy, the way we produce and distribute for ourselves all that we need, why is it that these instruments, recognisable as goods in common, are part of a system which is so violent and destructive of many human goods? Just as the butcher's sharp knife is a useful tool, which can be dangerous in the wrong hands, or when put to wrongful use, so also the instruments of market and capital can be in the wrong hands and badly used. This was recognised from the beginning of reflection on the phenomena of the economy.

Adam Smith in his renowned *Wealth of Nations* (first published in 1776) identified competition as an essential condition for markets to function for the common good. The alternative to competition is monopoly, and monopoly introduces distortions so that markets benefit some to the disadvantage of others. Competition in the economy is what we rely on to ensure efficiency, and it is the condition for why we can rely on markets to produce benefits for all.[1] Smith asked why it is that the activities of many different people operating independently of

---

1　Adam Smith, *An Inquiry into the Nature and Causes of the Wealth of Nations*, in two volumes, edited by R.H. Campbell and A.S. Skinner, Indianapolis: Liberty Fund, 1981, originally published 1776, p. 145.

one another somehow result in a coordinated order that was not planned by anybody but appeared as if it were. The spontaneous order Smith observed, he explained in terms of competition: under conditions of competition each provider of goods and services must ensure they are delivering quality of product at appropriate prices because if they don't, their customers will go to their competitors. It is often asserted that Smith claimed that the market can be relied upon to produce the common good in the sense of benefit to all. That is a distortion of his view. He only made the claim for competitive markets, not for any market. And what is more, he did not assume that all markets would naturally be competitive. On the contrary, he warned against the tendency of all merchants to create cartels, forming alliances with those who should be their competitors, so that they can find ways of 'fleecing the populace'.

Advocates of free markets rarely quote the following passages from Smith's book: 'People of the same trade seldom meet together, even for merriment and diversion, but the conversation ends in a conspiracy against the publick, or in some contrivance to raise prices.'[2] The market only functions beneficially so long as there is competition, so monopolising tendencies such as arise with the creation of cartels are a real threat to the public interest. Smith writes of the merchants as a group 'whose interest is never exactly the same with that of the publick, who have generally an interest to deceive and even to oppress the publick, and who accordingly have, upon many occasions, both deceived and oppressed it'.[3] (They have succeeded in doing this by influencing legislators to enact regulations of trade, which

---

2   Adam Smith, *Wealth of Nations*, p. 145.
3   Adam Smith, *Wealth of Nations*, p. 267.

secures their monopolies.) The enforcement of competition is one major reason why regulation of markets is warranted.

The tendency towards monopoly, the interest of the merchants in artificially increasing their own rewards from the market, must be resisted. So Smith argued that the public authorities must take steps to oblige the merchants to compete. Far from Adam Smith being a defender of unregulated markets, as is often asserted, he maintained that regulation was essential to protect the populace from being fleeced and to oblige the merchants to compete with one another.

Nowadays we are faced with many elements in markets which militate against the competition that guarantees efficiency. There are many ways in which businesses can secure an element of monopoly for themselves. Patents, licences, brand names and privileged location all distort competition and allow a dimension of monopoly to intrude. The effect of monopoly is to allow some to exploit their market position to enrich themselves at the expense of others, who need not bear such costs if there were more competition in the market.

As the butcher's knife is dangerous in the wrong hands, so too are markets dangerous when dominated by monopolists, or indeed, by monopsonists (those who dominate the buying side of markets, from monopsony a market situation in which there is only one buyer). Big supermarket chains can function as both when they are the only buyer for their suppliers, and so can force down the prices they pay to suppliers, since the suppliers have no alternative purchasers. Milk producers in Ireland and the UK complain about this phenomenon, which leaves them out of pocket, since the price they get from supermarket chains is insufficient to cover the production costs of the milk.

Markets in the wrong hands are dangerous, but whose hands are the wrong hands? In CST a key element of the teaching is the principle of the universal destination of material goods. In other words, all material wealth should be used to benefit humankind in general. That is the universal purpose, as distinct from the particular purpose which an owner of capital or of a business might have. Property should be so used that it benefits everyone. Unfortunately, we live in a world in which it is assumed that the right to private property entitles property owners to regard their resources as at their disposal for whatever purposes they desire, irrespective of the needs of the people around them. The Catholic tradition defends private property, but as a way of locating responsibility, and not entitlement, not an absolute right. The owner is the one with the responsibility to ensure that the goods in question are so used that the benefits accrue to many, not only to the owner. The exercise of such responsibility is a good in itself, allowing people to exercise control over their environment, and to show concern for their neighbours. Someone without property is deprived of this opportunity to exercise autonomy and responsibility. The accumulation of surplus translated into capital is a useful instrument, which might be used to benefit many. That it is used in practice to enrich a relative few counts as a great shame in terms of Church teaching.

The tragedy of our world is that many holders of assets of various kinds use these assets to increase their own wealth, and not to provide for their fellows in need. The tragedy is reinforced by the seeming rationality of this system; in other words, people defend their action or inaction by showing how irrational it would be to forego on the opportunities of gaining more wealth. In the face of such intransigence, talk of the common good is subversive. Admittedly, such talk cannot offer a clear solution that might be implemented immediately. But if the question is sufficiently raised and addressed by competent people, it is conceivable that we might discover another way of cooperating to provide for all people what is needed for a good life.

Chapter Six
Individualism

In the Monty Python film *Life of Brian*, there is a scene in which Brian is making one of his speeches, and he tells the crowd enthusiastically cheering him on: 'We are all individuals!' The audience responds with the chant: 'We are all individuals!' A lone voice from the back of the crowd pipes up: 'I'm not!'

I want to return to a topic we touched upon in the second chapter on goods and values, and which also came into our discussion of the economy and the common good. It has to do with self-interest, greed and avarice. In writing and speaking about common goods one constant source of difficulty for me has been the assumptions people make about what it is to be rational. These assumptions are reflected in all sorts of remarks that people make and in the kind of questions they ask. 'It's everyman for himself', 'what's in it for me?', 'you have to look out for yourself, because nobody else will do it for you'. The same assumptions make it difficult for my students and listeners to recognise the difference between having interests (being self-interested), and being selfish. So people wonder how, if we are all egoistic, we can be expected to be altruistic?

It is often assumed that the driving force behind the growing inequality in earnings, especially in the finance, banking and corporate sectors in which individuals demand not just big salaries but enormous bonuses, is greed. If we are trapped in a mindset which takes it as a given that everyone is out for him or herself, seeking one's own good, how then can there be common goods?

In coping with this assumption and the arguments grounded on it, I have often found myself trapped into sharing the presupposition, and then struggling to find a way out. So pervasive is this view of human beings that I find I am colonised by it also. We face a paradox: despite the reality we daily experience, we seem to be convinced it is something else! How can we accept a way of thinking which is supposed to make sense of our experience, but which is contradicted daily by our experience?

Every day parents and guardians care for their children, spouses and partners care and provide for each other, family members look after their sick and elderly, friends look out for one another, and so on. So familiar is this experience (note the word 'familiar': as close to us as family!) that we do not think twice about it. Beyond the confines of family and intimate friendship we recognise the extent to which our common life depends on people offering themselves for service to others, a service which at its heart cannot be recompensed with money. In charitable organisations, in clubs and societies, in sporting associations, in Church and religious communities, and in party and local politics, people get involved and take on work and responsibility, all of which brings costs and burdens as well as the satisfaction of seeing something good being achieved.

In our social and political lives, in which we depend on institutions such as parliaments and law courts, hospitals and schools, social welfare provision, not to mention the security services of armed forces and police, we benefit from the constructions of many people who themselves did not have the benefits which they hoped to make available to others. Pádraig Pearse can serve as an example from Irish history. Whatever judgement may be passed in retrospect on the actions he undertook in 1916, his motivation was to achieve something of benefit to later generations. As he formulated it in his poem 'The Fool':

[W]hat if the dream come true?
What if the dream come true? and if millions unborn shall dwell
In the house that I shaped in my heart, the noble house of my thought?

How many of the great pioneers in politics and society are deemed benefactors since their work and efforts and sacrifice have benefited many people? For instance, Martin Luther King, Pope John XXIII, the founding figures of the European movement that led to the EU, Jean Monnet, Robert Schuman, Alcide De Gasperi, among others. Every corporation and every institution has its memory of founders who are celebrated precisely because their efforts have left a legacy of benefit to later generations whom they could not have known.

Of course all of these people act for reasons, their own reasons. But it beggars belief to think that their reasons reduce to benefit for themselves. That the outcomes they strove for, universal franchise, equal pay for women, the old age pension, equal opportunity in access to healthcare, to education, are all to be explained in terms of pay-off to themselves? And yet that has become the dominant model of rationality operative in people's spontaneous thinking.

First of all, of course, we have to acknowledge that there might be a possibility of selfishness in everyone's actions. People can be tempted to take advantage of their position, to benefit themselves at the expense of others, to exploit their opportunities of enriching themselves whenever they can get away with it. Indeed, this is the motivation of crime, which in our world is systematically organised, not just locally but internationally. We have plenty of examples of it in Ireland: 'brown envelopes' changing hands in the local planning process; the scams exposed in property speculation and development; the bankers who allowed other people's money to be dispensed in purchase of overvalued property without collateral for the debt, now being administered by NAMA.

But isn't it a form of madness to think that the thought processes of criminals are the normal thought processes of human beings? That everyone is simply out for themselves and is willing to do whatever they can get away with if it will benefit them? This is what the general assumption of individual selfish rationality boils down to.

Everyone who acts has their own reasons for acting. To know what those reasons are, one would have to ask, and take time to listen and understand and perhaps challenge and investigate further. We know how difficult this can be and how prone we can be to misunderstand. Judicial investigations and sworn enquiries have difficulty coming to terms with what happened in the recent past and the reasons people had for the decisions they took. Human reasons are multiform and complex, and this makes the task of explanation difficult.

To simplify the task of explanation all sciences rely on forms of abstraction called idealisations. For instance, geometry defines a point in a plane as having position but no mass. A teacher's effort to illustrate this by a chalk mark on the blackboard might help, but essentially fails, because the chalk mark inevitably has a size, some mass. We are familiar with other idealisations, using phrases like 'all else being equal', or 'under laboratory conditions', or 'at standard temperature and pressure'. So when human scientists try to explain human behaviour they too resort to idealisations, formulating models which abstract from the particularities of any concrete situation and generalise to the kind of model we are familiar with from economics or rational choice theory. An agent is assumed to be motivated to maximise returns to self, and so will weigh the benefits and burdens of various options which are available to achieve some preferences. The 'correct' option is identified by the theory as that one which most effectively and efficiently realises the agent's preferences, in the best balance of benefits over costs. With this highly abstract model a theory can be elaborated which allows for the generation of hypotheses, which in turn can be tested in practice. Will the demand for petrol be affected by an increase in price due to added tax? Will additional national insurance charges added to the cost of employing people significantly affect the number of jobs on offer? These questions can be answered by checking performance in markets following the changes. However, confirmation of the hypothesis in experience might reinforce the theory as useful, but it does not make the abstracted model of choice at the heart of the theory any more likely to be an accurate account of what goes on in anyone's decision-making.

Some people might believe that the way to be rational is the way imagined in the models used by economics and rational choice theory. Contrary to our experience, which shows us many ways of being rational, our minds and our language have been colonised by this single idea that to be rational is to be a bargain hunter, pursuing our goals as individuals, always seeking to cut costs and to increase pay-offs to ourselves. While, undoubtedly, there are contexts in which this model is relevant, the point here is to challenge its adoption as the only model to guide our decisions and actions.

Sciences, including human sciences, proceed by simplifying, by abstracting from the complexity of real life so as to find some explanations which might 'for the most part', or 'under ideal conditions', prove useful. And that is perfectly valid as long as we remember that the basic model is a simplification, an idealisation. It works for science, but not for practical wisdom. Practical wisdom must not lose sight of the complexity and must give it its due.

The simple single term 'interest' can conceal the complexity unless we bear in mind how many kinds of interest people can have and how their interest can be in benefit to others as much as to themselves. I have often noticed how easily students assume that to speak of someone pursuing their interests is to accuse them of selfishness. They identify self-interest with selfishness. But it is not necessarily selfish to have and pursue self-interest. Aunt Jane on a visit brings sweets and chocolates for her nieces and nephews. Each of the children has an interest in those goodies – very naturally and healthily. But any child that wants more than their fair share, or most radically, that wants to have all the sweets for themself, is selfish.

What then should be the attitude of those committed to common goods towards greed? Does commitment to the perspective of common goods require the condemnation of greed? This is not a simple question. It is one thing to recognise the distorting effect of avarice, selfishness and greed on a person's character and moral life; it is another matter altogether to think that social and political problems such as the 2007/08 sub-prime mortgage market collapse can be explained solely in terms of the personal vices of individual persons. As noted above with regard to rationality, a whole culture's way of thinking can be distorted, and it may be possible to explain social catastrophe in terms of shared blindness, wrongheadedness or shared stupidity. If we recruit our brightest graduates into the banking and financial sector and encourage them to take risks, and reward their risk-taking with enormous bonus payments, and celebrate the results when shareholders get dividends and property owners find the value of their assets increases, then it doesn't make sense to say the personal greed of the bankers is to blame when the system implodes. Social approval was abundantly available for the new way of doing business after deregulation. As noted above, Pope Paul VI in *Evangelii Nuntiandi* stressed we must pay attention not only to the personal faults of individuals in need of conversion, but we must examine our collective conscience, our shared values and common perspectives, to recognise their need for conversion also.

Journalistic commentary on the financial and banking crises of 2007/08 has frequently pointed to the greed of bankers and traders as a cause of the bubble that finally burst. This was far too convenient as an explanation, and dangerously simple as a location of the blame. But it had its attraction for a public that was reeling in shock from the experience of seeing savings jeopardised if not lost, pension funds in danger of evaporation and the housing market collapsing, leaving many holding negative equity, debts to be repaid which far exceed the present value of the properties. The taxpayers who are called upon to bail out banks and financial institutions want to be able to point the finger, to identify a culprit on whom the blame can be laid. The greed of certain individuals offers a convenient candidate, and the media are well able to oblige.

There are convenient Hollywood images available for the purpose of assigning blame. The character of Gordon Gekko, played in the film *Wall Street* by Michael Douglas, is taken to typify a certain kind of exploitative trader who is unconstrained by moral concerns in the pursuit of wealth. His speech before a meeting of shareholders in which he propounds 'greed is good' stands for the political ideology of the 1980s when the politics of Margaret Thatcher and Ronald Reagan strove to deregulate markets and facilitate the unhindered pursuit of wealth.

Human desires reveal a broad range, and some desires can degenerate into greed unless held in tension by compassion and the commitment to justice. When desire is so degenerated, it warrants condemnation. *The Catechism of the Catholic Church* comments along these lines. But it is also interesting to note that the various documents in the tradition of CST that highlight injustice and condemn the circumstances in which people are exploited or condemned to live in conditions that are unworthy of human beings seldom regard greed as such as the cause of these great wrongs.

Pope Pius XI's *Quadragesimo Anno*, 'On Reconstruction of the Social Order' (1931), published just after the crisis of the Wall Street Crash of 1929, affirms:

Those who are engaged in production are not forbidden to increase their fortunes in a lawful and just manner: indeed it is just that he who renders service to society and develops its wealth should himself have his proportionate share of the increased public riches, provided always that he respects the law of God and the rights of his neighbour, and uses his property in accord with faith and right reason. If these principles be observed by all, everywhere and at all times, not merely the production and acquisition of goods, but also the use of wealth, now so often uncontrolled, will within a short time be brought back again to the standards of equity and just distribution. (*QA*, 136)

There are several themes in this brief passage which resonate throughout the encyclical letter, and indeed throughout the tradition of Catholic social thought. First, it is clear that there is no rejection in principle of the pursuit of wealth, the desire for gain or profit, as if these were wrong in themselves. Second, there are certain conditions that must obtain, if the pursuit of wealth is to be in harmony with the divine will. Third, the pursuit of wealth goes out of control when these conditions are neglected, or inadequately incorporated in regulation. Hence, fourth, greed does not name a cause of the problem, but in its social impact a consequence of a different problem which might be called the absence of due order.

There are remarkable parallels between the crisis analysed in *Quadragesimo Anno* and our twenty-first century crisis. The word 'globalisation' is not used but the global influence of capitalism is recognised (QA, 103). A weakness of this encyclical is that it speaks about justice, good order, equity and appropriate shares as belonging to the divinely willed plan for society, as if there were some way of consulting the will of God in making the distribution. In the absence of a blueprint, which prescribes the amount of fair shares, the capitalist system relies on the market to allocate efficiently what is due to each. The danger then is that those who benefit hugely in the distribution can reassure themselves that they are entitled to what they get, regardless of what others obtain, because the allocation is supposedly made in an impersonal and fair way by the system. That is, of course, presuming the market system operates with the conditions of open competition. Pius XI did not think those conditions were met: 'Free competition has committed suicide; economic dictatorship has replaced a free market' (*QA*, 109).

It is notable that Pope Pius XI does not react to the crisis of his day by condemning greed, ambition for power, or other distorted motives. Instead he sees the solution in a reordering of goods (*QA*, 136). Created, temporal and human-made goods are genuinely good and worth pursuing as long as they contribute to a harmonious pursuit of the ultimate good. Where this integrating context is lacking, where there is no standard of a higher good with which to measure the enjoyment of the lesser good, the danger is that the limited good will take the place of the unrestricted and infinite good which is God. Conscience is the capacity in humans to make that practical judgement about the appropriateness of pursuing particular goods relative to the highest good. When it is silenced, then there is no restraint on human avarice when it is encouraged by an ideology that advocates unrestricted market freedoms and by corresponding regulatory structures which allow acquisitiveness free rein. And so the Pope concludes:

As a result, a much greater number than ever before, solely concerned with adding to their wealth by any means whatsoever, sought their own selfish interests above all things; they had no scruple in committing the gravest injustices against others. Those who first entered upon this broad way which leads to destruction easily found many imitators of their iniquity because of their manifest success, their extravagant display of wealth, their derision of the scruples of more delicate consciences and the crushing of more cautious competitors. (*QA*, 134)

The role of the state is critical in fostering justice and the common good. To this end, the Pope suggests, 'free competition, and especially economic domination, must be kept within definite and proper bounds, and must be brought under effective control of the public authority, in matters pertaining to the latter's competence' (*QA*, 110). His repeated recommendation that the state exercise an appropriate control over the economy is not formulated in terms of mastering greed, or restraining avarice or envy. Instead, as in this instance, it is a matter of regulating social and economic institutions such as the market based on free competition. It is the failure to regulate those institutions, and in recent history the deregulation that removed controls on financial institutions, that allows scope for greed, unbridled ambition, envy and selfish possessiveness to find expression and appear to be successful. The source of the problem is not the greed, but the absence of a disciplined regime in which greed might be kept in check and the pursuit of genuine goods for all could be fostered.

The emphasis on the proper order of goods continues through the later documents in the tradition. Pope John

Paul II took up this theme in his encyclical letter *Centesimus Annus* (1991) marking the centenary of *Rerum Novarum*, 'Revolutionary Change'. The Pope focuses on consumerism as the culture which elevates instrumental goods to the position of the ultimate good. 'It is not wrong to want to live better; what is wrong is a style of life which is presumed to be better when it is directed towards "having" rather than "being", and which wants to have more, not in order to be more but in order to spend life in enjoyment as an end in itself' (*CA*, 36). In this letter he asks whether capitalism might be recommended as a model to developing countries searching for the path to true economic and civil progress. It is worth quoting his answer at length:

> If by capitalism is meant an economic system which recognises the fundamental and positive role of business, the market, private property and the resulting responsibility for the means of production, as well as free human creativity in the economic sector, then the answer is certainly in the affirmative, even though it would perhaps be more appropriate to speak of a business economy, market economy or simply free economy. But if by capitalism is meant a system in which freedom in the economic sector is not circumscribed within a strong judicial framework which places it at the service of human freedom in its totality, and which sees it as a particular aspect of that freedom, the core of which is ethical and religious, then the reply is certainly negative. (*CA*, 42)

A strong judicial framework is one which sufficiently regulates economic activity so that it is both fostered and constrained. Economic activity is to be fostered, because of its effectiveness in providing real goods and services for societies; it is to be constrained, because of the dangers of wastefulness, harm and injustice associated with uncontrolled markets. Reliance on an adequate regulation could free participants in markets from having to make an ethical investigation and decision on each particular issue that arises. The absence of such regulation means that those who know and understand what is going on release themselves from responsibility. They simply point to the obligations of the regulatory authorities and the ethics commissions, and in the absence of directives they conclude they are free to do whatever is not forbidden.

This survey from Catholic social thought shows that the tradition of reflection on economic and social reality does not place the blame for failures and crises on the greed of some individuals. Instead, the perspective is wider, looking to the shared meanings and values of a society and the ways in which these hinder or foster institutions which contribute to the good life. When our society treats monetary reward as the only meaningful acknowledgment of excellence, and communicates to its young bankers, professionals and entrepreneurs, that they should consider themselves as successful only when their bonus allows them to flaunt a Maserati or a Porsche, then it is too easy to say the problem is greed, and not rather the conventional standards for recognising achievement. It doesn't always have to be a financial reward for excellence, as we see in the amateur sports trophies, the literature prizes, the honours for civic service, or the medals for exemplary military courage or initiative.

The good life is one lived in accord with a true order of goods, in which created and temporal goods are relativised. Flawed institutions and the failure to regulate them properly provide scope for the disordered desires of some to find encouragement and expression. The apparent success of those who break through the constraints of good order and the moral law gives example to the more timid and an incentive to do likewise.

Furthermore, the style of reflection exemplified in this aspect of the Catholic Church's tradition grounds a suspicion that the tendency to seek out a single factor for blame in the context of such a wide social phenomenon functions to conceal the responsibility of many others in the society. Those who have benefited to date from disordered structures, including assumptions about what is natural and unchangeable, have a vested interest in distracting attention from these structures, and in fostering the public outcry against the greed of individuals. An example in the Irish case is how the print media colluded in the fostering of a property bubble by carrying extensive property supplements in the newspapers. As always commercial media can defend their performance by claiming that they only provide what their readers want. If the readers don't want the news about property values, they won't buy the papers. Of course, that is true, but it only underlines the point. It is the social acceptability of making a fetish of property, shared by publishers and consumers alike, that sustains the risk-taking in the financial and banking sector, since the risks prove effective, in the short run, for boosting property values. A critical, reflective examination of the operative values was not possible while the dance was on and the music was playing. And the print and broadcast media were not in a position to offer the relevant reflection while they contributed their own drumming to the music.

In this chapter I have returned to an issue mentioned in chapter two about the distortions that can arise from simplified models. This was necessary to counter a popular response to the problems of inequality identified in the last chapter on the economy, to clarify that our difficulties cannot be blamed on individuals' greed alone. The shared meanings and values are essential to the common good of any community, and if those meanings and values encourage excess, then the common good is at risk. If unregulated wealth creation is seen as the strategy for development then we should not wonder when the resulting inequality and disregard for those left stranded undermines all sense of communality and solidarity. Whether or not my argument is persuasive, I suggest that it can serve as a useful illustration of the kind of examination of collective conscience that Pope Paul VI called for in his exhortation on evangelisation, outlined in chapter four. According to *Evangelii Nuntiandi*, 'Evangelisation in the Modern World', evangelisation is a matter of 'affecting and as it were upsetting, through the power of the Gospel, mankind's criteria of judgement, determining values, points of interest, lines of thought, sources of inspiration and models of life, which are in contrast with the Word of God and the plan of salvation' (*EN*, 19). Individualism, whether the focus on the interests or the faults of individual people, belongs among the determining models of our world in need of conversion.

Chapter Seven
Common Goods and Human Rights

Many people are suspicious of any talk of the common good because they fear that authorities are about to use the rhetoric of common goods to coerce them to conform to someone else's view of how they should live their lives. They don't want any such vision of the good imposed upon them, but desire to be free to choose their own life goals. This is the truly positive aspect of individualism. Autonomy, the freedom to direct one's own life according to one's own appreciation of what is good and worthwhile, is the dominant value in our time. And it is autonomy that is seen to be threatened by talk of the common good. Autonomy is the value protected in various rights: to freedom of conscience and speech, to freedom of association, to freedom of movement and freedom from discrimination. People typically express their anxiety by pointing out that various tyrannical regimes appealed to the common good when forcing conformity on their peoples. Hitler and Stalin are taken as representatives of extreme views of common goods, namely, German nationalism, and Soviet communism. Are human rights in tension with common goods?

Of course it is the case that tyrants have abused the language of morals and politics. Not only the common good, but virtues such as: fidelity, loyalty, generosity, obedience, diligence, equality and liberty have been pressed into service of reprehensible regimes. There is nothing specific about the concept of common good as distinct from any other moral vocabulary to make it prone to abuse. The Nazis were 'National Socialists'; should it follow, therefore, that no one who claims to be a nationalist or even a socialist could be trusted, and must indeed be suspected of attempting to hijack the political system in the name of a terrible agenda?

It would be foolish to attempt to deny the abuse of the language of common goods, and the abuse of people in the name of common goods. The term can be misused in such a way that the common good is by definition intrinsically hostile to the freedom and self-determination of individuals. Their membership of the relevant group is supposed to commit people to the good of the group as a whole, and that good is not determined through a process of deliberation and debate but is pre-given. It may be thought to be determined by nature or by tradition (the national interest or shared values of the cultural and ethnic group) or some other way that overrides individuals' rights to contribute to the process.

Families come in many shapes and sizes, and we know how oppressive they can be. History provides specific examples of families in which the dynastic interests of maintaining ownership of estates or rule in male succession predominated over all other possible values, to the detriment of persons and relationships. Cultures that allow honour killings of daughters or wives who are considered to have violated the honour of their families provide examples of such a notion of the common good of the family that it may override the good, even the life and existence of individual members. The cultural norms which carry a society's expectation of marriage and the family and the roles within them can be experienced as oppressive, and insofar as the cultural norm is advocated in terms of the common good, then the common good as the predetermined good of an organic whole will be experienced as oppressive. It cannot be denied that appeals to nature, or to values, or to tradition, or other such authoritative sources of meaning for the common good have been used to oppress people and to deprive them of the opportunity of questioning inherited assumptions and of contributing to reshaping communal projects.

The irony is that the analysis of common good provides the correctives to any such abuse of the language whereby it might appear to justify the oppression of individuals in the name of the good of the whole. These correctives can be found at least in a primitive form in the writings of Aristotle, who pioneered the philosophical reflection on common goods. Aristotle claims that as all action is for a good, so all cooperation is for a good in common. He then goes on to claim that the highest form of cooperation is for the highest common good. This he understood to be political, that is, the collaboration of citizens in caring for the quality of their characters and the quality of their life together in a city such as Athens.

There are various reasons why it doesn't make sense to speak of our political entities (states such as Ireland, UK, France, the EU) as aiming at a common good, much less the highest possible good. One obvious reason is that conflict is a central part of our experience of politics, and the activity of politics is the attempt to find conciliation between opposing interests. The political way of managing conflict (I don't say resolving:

it is seldom that our conflicts at this level are resolved, but they are managed or handled politically) is to negotiate a settlement, conciliating opposing interests, and via compromise allowing all participants the possibility of being satisfied by the arrangement. No settlement is final; there is always the possibility of revisiting and revising the deals as new experiences and situations require.

Another reason for scepticism about Aristotle's view of the good is his teleology, which finds little resonance in the contemporary context. This is the idea that there is a pre-given *telos* or ultimate purpose for human persons and for human communities commensurate with human nature. Contemporary political culture, so committed to the value of autonomy, is uncomfortable with the idea that people's goods or goals are prescribed to them by their nature. That seems to deny the real freedom people have in choosing their life-goals.

Both challenges can be turned by relying on the idea of *heuristic* to understand common good. A heuristic device is an aid to discovery. It is like the 'x' in algebra which allows us to name that which is to be discovered, even though we don't yet know what it is. The common good is what we are striving to discover; it names what we are searching for. The assumption is that there is a process of learning grounded in some context in which some things are known and in which meaningful questions can be formulated. The questions point beyond what is already known towards what is yet to be discovered. Some things are known about it, and indeed, enough is known about it to enable us to rule out unsatisfactory answers to the question. The idea of heuristic is rooted, therefore, in a process of learning, of discovery.

The processes of learning and discovery I have in mind take place through human history, not in the laboratory or the classroom. See, for instance, the learning process involved in overcoming slavery, a process which is not yet complete. See also the various forms of discrimination that had been taken for granted in the past as proper and right, but now are the very essence of injustice: discrimination against whatever groups of people have been labelled as 'other': non-Europeans, non-Christians, non-whites, non-males, non-heterosexuals. Racial, tribal, sexual, religious and political discrimination we have gradually learned to avoid and correct. In particular, in the political realm there has been a process of learning to manage conflict by means other than by the use of force, and so we have parliaments and congresses in which the enemies in former civil wars now confront each other in a debating chamber. The learning is not universal, it is not stable, and there is considerable fragility in this veneer of civility which has been achieved. Regression continues to be a possibility. The point here is to highlight the learning process of humanity, and in that process it is useful to have signposts, which point in the right direction. A heuristic does that.

The two main objections to Aristotle can be overcome with use of the idea of heuristic. With regard to human nature and the teleological understanding of what would constitute human fulfilment, we can deny that naming human nature or the human telos commits us to a particular understanding of that nature or that ultimate purpose. This was the hubris of the past in giving the impression that those who spoke of human nature were already in possession of an adequate comprehension of that nature. We are still in the process of discovery of what humans are capable of, and feats of achievement in individual excellence as well as in communal effort extend our horizons of the possible. As we discover more and more what humans are capable of, so our knowledge of human nature is expanded. The label 'nature' is a heuristic pointing to what we are discovering about ourselves and our capacities.

The other objection noted the prevalence of conflict in our political affairs and this motivated the denial of a common good. But if our politics is oriented to managing our conflicts in a certain way, then there is a dynamism pointed in a direction, and while we are a long way distant from the end goal of that dynamism, we can name it as the comprehensive set of solutions to our challenges of managing conflict. The common good of political life is a heuristic device identifying something we hope to discover, but do not yet know.

As noted, we do know some things, and these give us the resources for formulating criteria which we can apply in testing possible solutions. I formulate two criteria reconstructing the conditions that Aristotle used in evaluating different forms of constitution. Recall that in his view constitutions incorporate a vision of the good life and corresponding notions of justice and of friendly relations. But these two criteria can be derived analytically from the concept of common good also. If the goal is to be a *common* good, then it could only be such if it does not systematically exclude any individual or any group of persons from a fair share in the good for the sake of which we cooperate. This is the first criterion, modelled on Aristotle's concern that rule be for the good of all, and not merely for the good of the rulers, whether one, few, or many. And if the goal is to be a common *good*, then it could only be such if it does not systematically exclude or denigrate any genuine dimension of the human good. This second criterion is modelled on Aristotle's evaluation of different constitutions in terms of their conceptions of human good, whether expansive or constricted.

He relied on the phrase translated as 'always more than' to identify the conception of the human good which would be satisfactory and comprehensive; it would be always more than a mutual guarantee of rights, or a set of non-aggression pacts, or treaties to exchange goods and services. Pointing beyond has the aura of a heuristic about it, and even the attempts to spell out the contents of the good, the good life as more than life itself, noble actions, excellence in the performance of distinctive human activities such as friendship and justice, leave more unsaid than they actually manage to say.

These two criteria articulate the rationality of what is already intrinsic to our debates and our procedures. As noted above, our political culture has become highly sensitised to exclusion, and tendencies to exclude, and that corresponds to the application of the first criterion. The second criterion is more contentious, because it is implicit in many real disputes going on at present. With regard to educational policy, for instance, we are familiar with the demand that the physical well-being of pupils be a focus of attention and not only their intellectual development. So a balanced curriculum should include sports or PE. Consider also the debates in relation to sex education in schools, or the role of religion in the curriculum. Some people are concerned about the possible neglect of real dimensions of human good because of an exaggerated focus on other dimensions.

The notion of heuristic and the two criteria formulated philosophically find their parallels in Catholic social teaching. The two criteria, for instance, map very neatly onto the articulation by Pope Paul VI in his letter in 1967 *Populorum Progressio*, 'On the Development of Peoples', of what is involved in the pursuit of the common good: 'the integral development of every person, and of the whole person'. The fulfilment of every person: that's the first criterion than no one be excluded; integral fulfilment of the whole person: that's the second criterion, that no dimension of human well-being be systematically excluded from our shared concerns in social collaboration. These criteria find other articulations also in CST, as for instance when the focus is on the groups most likely to be excluded, namely, the poor and the marginalised, and so the Church authorities express their concern in terms of a preferential option for the poor. Pope Francis's letter in 2015 *Laudato Si'*, 'Care for our Common Home', is one example of the use of the second criterion as dimensions of well-being are in danger of being neglected in the context of the challenges of climate change and environmental degradation.

Also in the literature of CST we find the notion of heuristic implicit in the formulations used for speaking of the ultimate goals of human life, 'integral fulfilment'. This term is never exhaustively defined. As with Aristotle, it is said to be always more than material sufficiency, or the absence of war. But the heuristic nature of the notion of fulfilment is acknowledged in the significant shift in the specification of the meaning of common good that we noted in chapter four. Pope John XXIII in his 1961 letter *Mater et Magistra*, 'Mother and Teacher', and subsequently in the Second Vatican Council's Pastoral Constitution in 1966, focused on conditions for human flourishing, not the ultimate common good. Especially in terms of the Vatican Council's *Gaudium et Spes*, the aspiration was to find, via dialogue, bases of collaboration between people with differing views of that ultimate fulfilment, that will enable them to work together to build a better world. We don't know in detail what that ultimate fulfilment will be – notions such as beatific vision, life in the resurrection, the sight of the

Glory of God on the face of Christ, put a name to it but don't describe it – and to the extent that we can name it, we don't find agreement with others about it. But, the Council hoped, it may be possible to find agreement on the conditions that would have to be met if people are to achieve their fulfilment, however we understand it.

Their human rights are among the conditions for the flourishing and fulfilment of individuals and groups identified by *Gaudium et Spes* and other important documents of CST. There are several dimensions to the link between human rights and common goods. Those who have seen the common good as a threat to their independence and freedom have stressed the importance of human rights as ensuring protection to individuals against overbearing and potentially oppressive public authorities. This way of characterising human rights is both satisfactory and unsatisfactory. It is indeed the case that the states which are the signatories to the various international conventions, as for instance the European Convention on Human Rights, agree to accept the listed rights as setting standards below which they will not fall in their treatment of their own citizens and residents. To that extent they are self-imposed constraints on what public authorities can do to and with citizens. However, the states are in an ambiguous position. On the one hand, the states themselves are seen as the greatest threat to individuals' rights; on the other hand, they themselves are the agents charged with upholding and vindicating those rights. Despite the ambiguous position of the states, as both threat and defender, it is a highly satisfactory depiction of human rights to consider them as constraints on state power, and as instruments for the protection of individuals. This is one positive link between common good and individuals' rights.

The unsatisfactory aspect of this depiction is that it is inclined to polarise individuals' rights and the common good and make them appear as opposed. This becomes a lazy way of thinking about problems when a policy designed to ensure the general welfare or the state's interest in public order is seen to jeopardise the freedoms of some individuals. The common good then appears as that which threatens rights, and rights are the assurances people have that their own interests will not be overridden in the name of public policy. Although convenient, this way of depicting the situation does not contribute to finding a solution.

As noted above, the language of common goods like other moral language can be misused, but it is not helpful to identify the terms only with their incorrect usage. The criteria which can make the notion of common good applicable in practice specify that any systematic exclusion of individuals or groups from a just share in the goods for the sake of which people cooperate would be contrary to the common good. The affirmation and promotion of human rights is a way of implementing this criterion. In this sense the regime of human rights is a common good of all the individuals whose interests are protected. It is a common good in the sense that each one has a reason to uphold and support the regime, and to cooperate with all others in making it work. In the basic sense in which cooperation is always for goods in common, the cooperation of our political communities in establishing and maintaining a human rights regime is for a common good. This is a second way in which rights and common good are positively linked, in that the regime of human rights belongs among the goods which citizens value and pursue together. This reality is denied or at least overlooked when the common good is characterised simply as potential threat to individuals' liberties.

A third linkage is in the comprehensive listing of the things to which people are said to have rights. The Universal Declaration of Human Rights adopted by the United Nations in 1948 had to be translated into various conventions so that its rights could become part of international law. Civil and political rights are distinguished from social and economic rights in the conventions, but still the goods at stake can be read as sketching all that would be desirable for a decent human existence, a life well lived. The second criterion, that no aspect of human good be systematically excluded from our consideration in our common activity, is reflected in this dimension of human rights language, the comprehensive perspective on human goods.

In the Catholic tradition of upholding the common good, the focus can be directly on those groups which are vulnerable to exploitation or discrimination – hence the adoption of the language of preferential option for the poor. The Church wants to place itself at the side of those who are victims, who suffer, who bear a disproportionate burden either as a result of natural catastrophe or human irresponsibility. Pope Francis is not the first modern pope to speak out against injustices and inequality – this has always been a theme in the speeches of the travelling popes in their various host countries. But Pope Francis has drawn attention to the plight of the migrants and refugees now arriving en masse on Europe's southern borders. His visit to Lampedusa early in the crisis (8 July 2013) and his subsequent visit to Greece (16 April 2016) drew attention to the urgency of the problem. This kind of prophetic action, as well as more considered statements, belong with the stance of solidarity, one of the key aspects of CST which is linked with the common good. In 1987 Pope John Paul II addressed it in *Sollicitudo rei socialis*, 'On Social Concern', as follows: 'solidarity is not a vague feeling of compassion, but a firm commitment to the common good, because we are all really responsible for all.' Solidarity is thus linked directly to the first criterion that none be excluded. It is the firm commitment to take the side of those who are vulnerable to exclusion, and an essential aspect of that in our modern world is to ensure that their human rights are upheld.

Human rights regimes, with conventions, courts, observers and activists apply what has already been formulated and officially adopted as binding law. However, with situations such as the flood of migrants and refugees, we see the limitations of what is already in place. Definitions of terms and agreed procedures (the so-called Dublin Regulation which required that asylum seekers be registered in the first country in which they arrive) proved incapable of application when the numbers of migrants coming from many different source countries overwhelmed the resources available to receive them. Solidarity now requires a firm commitment, not only to providing care for those in need as far as possible, but especially to devising new systems and updated procedures to ensure fairness and transparency in what is done. Where the Dublin Regulation had seemed to uphold the value of subsidiarity, the new system will have to find appropriate ways to ensure this important linked value in the common good.

The principle of subsidiarity insists that assistance motivated by solidarity should not replace the efforts of recipients themselves to address their problems and find solutions. It entails a willingness to help, with an expectation that those being helped take responsibility to find and implement their own solutions to their problems. In a hierarchically structured governance system the principle of subsidiarity requires that the higher level authorities assist but do not replace those operating on the ground. This is opposed to all centralising tendencies which are inclined to draw all power to the centre of institutions or organisations, depriving the so-called grass-roots of opportunities to manage their own affairs.

In his 2009 encyclical letter *Caritas in Veritate*, 'Charity in Truth', Pope Benedict writes: 'The principle of subsidiarity must remain closely linked to the principle of solidarity and vice versa, since the former without the latter gives way to social privatism, while the latter without the former gives way to paternalist social assistance that is demeaning to those in need' (*CV*, 58). I suppose by 'social privatism' the Pope means the attitude which says that everyone should be left alone to mind their own business, and by its opposite, 'paternalistic social assistance', he means the paternalistic attitude of acting on the assumption that one knows what is best for others. This statement is made originally in the context of reflection on international development aid. There are two important values which are to be respected, and disregard of one in favour of the other can lead to distorting or objectionable outcomes. Development aid goes beyond disaster relief, the provision of what is immediately and desperately needed in terms of clean water, food, shelter, and protection from disease. Development aid looks towards the future in the spirit of building infrastructure and systems to ensure the regular availability of life-sustaining and life-enhancing goods and services. Whether it be economic development, the creation of health and education systems, or the facilitation of good governance, such aid is not focused on immediate need but on longer-term prospects for a society. It is in such circumstances that Pope Benedict stressed the linkage of solidarity and subsidiarity.

Put simply, solidarity is what binds donors and beneficiaries in a sense of a common humanity with its typical vulnerabilities so that the plight of those in need of development is recognised by their benefactors with a sense of compassion. Again, simply put, subsidiarity is rooted in the respect for the autonomy of those in need of assistance so that whatever aid is given does not deprive people of the capacity to provide for themselves. The two values must be linked in whatever policy of development aid is pursued. Respect for the autonomy and responsibility of individuals and groups might result in their being left to fend for themselves, unless that respect is balanced by a real concern for their welfare. On the other hand, Benedict warns that concern for the welfare of others can become a form of paternalism, if it is not balanced by respect for their own responsibility to provide for themselves according to their own estimation of their needs. Hence the emphasis on pairing these two principles of solidarity and subsidiarity, which nonetheless remain in tension with one another. Hence, Pope Benedict's telling remark:

> The principle of subsidiarity must remain closely linked to the principle of solidarity and vice versa (*CV*, 58).

Chapter Eight
Democracy and Common Goods

Is democracy our common good? Although the question seems simple enough, looking for a 'yes, no, or partly' answer, it turns out to be much more complex than that. This chapter will unpack some of that complexity. This should help to clarify what we can say using the language of common goods, and how that might help us as a society and a political culture to function better. One initial clarification is to note the ambiguity in the question, and also in the possible answer. The question might be meant in two ways: considering democracy as a common good itself; and considering it as a way of identifying and deciding on our common goods. I have to ask the reader's patience at this point. This is the first of several distinctions I will need to introduce in order to map out the complexity I've mentioned, so I beg your indulgence in following my line of thought through the following reflections. At each step I am aware that the issues raised are controversial, and while I am confident I can defend the position I take up, I am sure I will not be able to persuade everyone. However, even those who will disagree with me will find the discussion useful, and so I don't hesitate in inviting everyone to join in the task.

Politics is the context of the question about common good and democracy, but what do we mean by politics? People often define politics as the contest to achieve power in a state, which includes the power of making law. I suggest we go to a deeper level and recognise politics as one way of managing social conflict. It is by no means the only way, and it may not even appear to be the most effective way of dealing with conflict. Conflict arises because the goals pursued by different people are mutually frustrating or incompatible. A united Ireland is incompatible with Northern Ireland remaining within the United Kingdom; privatised water is incompatible with public ownership. Conflict can be managed by one group or party succeeding in imposing its will on the other groups. This can occur through the actual use of or the threat of violence. However, although we have plenty of evidence of forceful domination through human history, experience shows that this is not an enduring or stable way to manage conflict.

The management of conflict is political when it renounces such primary reliance on coercion and attempts to achieve conciliation through negotiation, argument and persuasion. That word 'renounces' is easily typed, and perhaps also easily read, but we should not underestimate the enormous personal achievement involved in making the commitment to lay down the weapons and engage in negotiation. The achievement of the Belfast Agreement was such a moment in our recent history. My suggestion then is that while the political management of conflict usually occurs within a state, the key to politics is not primarily the state institutions, but the reliance on talking and persuasion to achieve some accommodation between conflicted parties. It follows that only some forms of state rule are political in the proper sense. There are many forms of rule that either deny the reality and inevitability of conflict or attempt to eliminate or resolve conflict by force. Of course, the importance of the distinction does not entail that there can be a complete separation of these elements. Every state to survive must claim a monopoly on the legitimate use of coercive force within its territory.

The political management of conflict will usually involve compromise. Not every party to a conflict can achieve the realisation of all its goals – otherwise there would not have been a conflict in the first place. This is one reason to speak of managing instead of resolving conflict. Conflict persists, but the achievement of politics is that the conflict is conducted by talking rather than with the use of force. Only where there is a willingness on all sides to forego or postpone the achievement of some of their objectives can political accommodation be reached.

Conflict is understood in terms of incompatible goals. Goals are to be distinguished from ideals and values, as discussed in previous chapters. A goal is a state of affairs which one hopes to bring about, for example, free healthcare at the point of delivery. The state of affairs is capable of being described in all relevant features. By contrast, ideals or values such as justice, or peace, or compassion, can be invoked to make sense of one's motivation for wanting to bring about the quality of healthcare envisaged. Of themselves, the ideals or values are not capable of such precise description as is the case with goals.

Notoriously, people on opposite sides of a conflict can claim justice or peace or similar values to make sense of their position. Litigants who resort to courts hope to get justice, but until the court has decided the issue, parties in dispute presume that justice in the case lies with them. The point here is not to affirm that courts always succeed in doing justice; there are too many examples of blatant miscarriages of justice to make that case. Rather, the point is that many who invoke justice do not agree about what arrangements would be just: the appeal to justice does not provide common ground. Conflict is not resolved simply by parties in dispute espousing values and ideals such as justice. The language of values and ideals is aspirational, and it is not necessarily helpful for managing conflict. In fact, it can hinder the political dealing with conflict because an apparent agreement at the level of ideals may obscure the real differences of interests in what is proposed. For example, those who advocate the nationalisation of the banks are opposed by free market proponents, but both sides make their case in terms of what is conducive to the good of the economy and the common good. Reference to the values of the public welfare or the common good does not decide the issue in favour of one or other goal.

Good people wanting to do good things are in conflict with one another, because the goals they pursue are incompatible. For instance, cabinet ministers seeking more resources for their departments are in conflict. More money for education means less for security, or social welfare, or health. Conflict occurs because of the richness of the human good, the creativity of human agents, and the limitations of time, energy and material resources for them to realise their objectives. Of course, conflict also occurs because of greed, hatred, and the drive to dominate others. It is an important corrective for religious world views, however, to accept that conflict can also arise from good people wanting to do good things.

Most religious visions with their associated ideals favour harmony, community, peace, between the Creator and creatures, between all humankind, all peoples and states, and between humans and the rest of creation. Christian rhetoric often appeals to values, ideals, and visions of the good, easily evoked by powerful symbols from the Bible, such as beating swords into ploughshares, the heavenly banquet, the feeding of the multitude, and the healing of the blind and lame. But the relevant values and ideals cannot tell governments or other authorities what would be suitable policies to realise those ideals. Invoking ideals should not distract from or frustrate the work of building viable proposals based on reliable practical knowledge of the issues. On one hand, one danger is that religious language denies the reality of conflict, stressing instead the aspiration to harmony. On the other hand, another danger is that religious language exacerbates conflict and polarises the parties.

We have explored the meaning of politics, situating it in the context of conflict, and we have seen how conflict is basically about people wanting different or incompatible things (of course, conflict usually involves disagreement, but disagreement is not necessarily conflict). We have seen the importance of a commitment to manage conflict by talking which requires also a renunciation of reliance on force. The question remains: where does democracy fit in?

Where there is conflict, there is no consensus about what is to be done. Democracy is a way of making a decision in a society in the absence of consensus. We know of other ways that societies have made decisions in the absence of consensus. For instance, they have left the decision-making to an individual, publicly charged with the authority and responsibility to do so, an emperor, queen, or matriarch. The democratic way is to count votes, and allow the option favoured by the majority to succeed. It follows that the minority's preference is rejected. While democracy is required because of the absence of consensus, perhaps it can only work because there is at least a tacit consensus that the democratic way is the best way of managing the conflict, and this tacit consensus is fragile. The individuals affected, especially the losing minority, accept that the democratic choice is authoritative and binding.

Our societies attempt to reinforce the authoritative nature of the majority decision by using the rhetoric of 'The People'. Invoking the tacit consensus to abide by majority rule, the actual decision is said to be the decision, not of the majority, but of 'The People'. In actual fact, as we've seen in many referenda in Ireland, and in the June 2016 Brexit referendum in the UK, the outcome depends on levels of turnout, and on the swing-vote of a relatively small number of individuals, so it can be a mystification to attribute the decisions taken to some exalted entity such as 'The People'. All the more so in democratic systems such as that in the USA where there is a difference between the popular vote and the electoral college, or in the UK where the 'first past the post' system in constituencies can result in a government being formed without a majority of the popular vote.

Why would a minority accept the decision of the majority? After all, power in the hands of a majority is a dangerous weapon, capable of oppressing minorities, just as much as power in the hands of an autocrat, a tyrannical single individual, is capable of oppressing the whole people. The tyranny of the majority is always a possibility and the phrase summarises the reasons why many resisted the adoption of democratic forms of rule. So why would the defeated side in a vote accept the outcome with good grace? One reason given is that while any individual might find herself on the minority side on one issue, she is likely to find herself on the majority side on other issues. Another reason points to the constitutional constraints that impose limits on the power available to majorities. Such limits include the rights and liberties of individuals that may not be infringed by state power acting on behalf of a majority. These reasons don't always convince, especially in such cases as in Northern Ireland for many decades, where the minority found itself in a constructed minority, without any prospect of forming a majority, and at the same time deprived of important civil rights.

It is an extraordinary cultural achievement when citizens are convinced by the reasons for accepting majority rule and people are willing to accept defeat, without thereby losing their dignity or sense of self-worth. Where this cultural achievement is lacking, we find rulers and governments unable to expose themselves to rejection by popular vote and unable to relinquish power. This in turn becomes one of the great arguments in favour of democracy, that it enables electorates to remove unwanted or unsuccessful governments. Too often this feature of democracy is considered as desirable (in Iraq or Syria, for instance), without acknowledgement of the preconditions in the cultural achievement that might sustain democracy.

But before turning to the question about democracy and common goods, we need to consider one further distinction. This is the very familiar distinction between direct and representative democracy. If democracy is about making decisions in the absence of consensus, there are questions about who has a say in making the decisions, and there is another question about the kinds of decisions that are to be made. Every democracy will draw lines, construct borders which specify who has a say, usually in the form of a vote. 'All citizens aged

18 or over, resident in the country' is one possible and familiar demarcation. Where everyone meeting this specification is entitled to a say and vote on every issue, there is direct democracy. The decision is always taken by a majority of those 'present and voting'. This was the Greek experience of democracy (with the franchise confined to male property owners), and also of the Swiss Cantons to a large extent. This system can work with a relatively small electorate, and where issues are relatively simple, not requiring mastery of complex information and arguments. Sports clubs and local organisations provide other possible examples of direct democracy.

Our modern forms of democracy retain something of direct democracy in the practice of holding referenda. Our experience illustrates the requirement that issues be relatively simple, capable of being formulated in a yes/no option on the ballot paper. The referendum on the Eighth Amendment in Ireland illustrated the difficulty in getting the formulation right, and the subsequent referenda exposed the complexity of interpreting the result. The Brexit referendum in the UK is a similar instance in which the formulation was extremely simple, but subsequently there is great confusion about what exactly was meant or decided.

Given the great size of modern societies and the relative complexity of issues to be decided, representative democracy is the preferred form. This involves an electorate choosing delegates who are commissioned to take on the further tasks of deciding on laws and policies. The deputies meet in parliament or congress and from their own number elect officers, or, as in the US presidential system, vote to accept or reject officers proposed to them by the president. At local constituency level, voters select between candidates proposed to them by various political parties or independent individuals who offer themselves for election.

While the most common form of democracy is representative, the rhetoric of democracy remains rooted in the experience of direct democracy. This creates a tension to the extent that voters expect to have a say in the decisions made, but the only real say they have is in the remote selection of delegates, who in turn may or may not have a say in the selection of officers, who will formulate policy and propose it to parliament. Representative democracy requires these layers even to implement the outcome of a referendum, but still the rhetoric of democracy appeals to the will of 'The People'. The disjoint between the rhetoric and the reality is considerable, but somehow our political culture can live with it. The tensions remain, however, and are the source of considerable frustration.

The role of public opinion in relation to political decision-making should be mentioned here, since this is also a possibility for people to have a say. Chapter nine, 'Education as Common Good', will return to this theme while addressing the contribution of education to maintaining the public good of a political culture.

Is it for the common good that we have democratic government? This is the question we started with, and should now return to, having seen the complexity involved in appreciating what democracy is in practice. Clearly, it is a good thing for a society to have a way of managing conflict and all those who have come to appreciate the importance of managing conflict in a political manner, by talking and negotiating, instead of imposing the will of the more powerful, can share the common good of a democratic political system. Not everyone who claims to be a democrat will value democratic structures in this way. Some will endorse democracy only to the extent that it enables them to achieve their own goals, but democracy requires the willingness to compromise, and those who are unwilling to do so will have only a qualified commitment to democratic structures as a common good. As noted above, it is a considerable cultural achievement for a society to come to the point where it can manage its conflicts without resorting to force based on a shared willingness to conciliate.

We can now understand how the rhetoric of 'The People' is not a mere mystification, but can be an appeal to the shared acceptance of the democratic process. The existence of such a shared meaning among the citizen body as well as the continued efforts to renew and sustain the shared commitment to democracy is a common good of such a society. Democracy both in the sense of the structures needed and in the sense of the presupposed shared meaning and commitment is definitely a precious but also fragile common good. To be united in valuing and appreciating democracy does not require of an electorate that it be united on other bases, such as ethnicity or religious affiliation.

Our question of democracy and the common good also recognised the issue whether democracy was a good way of specifying common goods. There is a danger that we presume that we, or someone, know in advance what the common good is and what it requires. In politics we do not have the benefit of a pre-made template or a list of correct ingredients to ensure that everything turns out as planned. There is conflict with regard to the outcomes and conflict about the means. Nobody knows in advance what the best outcome would be and even if they did in some sense, we still find we don't know the best way of getting there. The reality of conflict, groups pursuing incompatible or mutually frustrating goals, means that there is no ultimate good which all groups can endorse in terms of which their conflict can be resolved. Each position can advocate on behalf of its vision and defend it in the language of common goods, but it remains the case that the two (or more) positions are not in agreement about their common good.

This is why we need democracy as a way of getting decisions made in the absence of consensus. It follows that the decisions taken can continue to be challenged as to the extent to which they actually realise common goods. This is typical of conflict being managed and not resolved. The experience of industrial relations has been a context of learning about managing conflict. In the nature of the case there is a disparity of interest between employees and employers: workers can have good reason to make their case for a greater share of the benefits of the common effort. Industrial disputes can be about matters other than pay: working conditions, health and safety issues, and terms of contract can also be the locus of conflict. Can we say in advance of a settlement what the common good requires? We can certainly affirm that some resolution is required by the common good, all the more so if the dispute negatively affects stakeholders such as the travelling public or consumers of energy, goods or services. But it is rarely the case that the just outcome can be sketched in detail in advance. The process of negotiation or perhaps arbitration is required to bring about some settlement, usually involving some compromise on both sides. Normally we can say it is good when the dispute is ended, but the actual resolution may well turn out to be flawed, and the dispute erupts again later. The process of managing the conflict is headed in a direction but in advance of a final settlement it is difficult to know what the just outcome would be. The process is oriented to finding the common good in a conflicted situation, something that will satisfy the legitimate concerns of all the stakeholders, particularly the parties in dispute.

Democracy as a process for managing conflict in the absence of consensus is also oriented to finding common goods, in relation to all the matters that are typically represented at a cabinet table: security, law and order, healthcare, education, the economy, business and work, relations with other states, and in pluralist societies community cohesion. The common good is to be discovered, and worked out in detail as issues are addressed and solutions sought. Democracy does seem to be a good way of finding goods that are common and that can be endorsed by all affected persons, because it offers some measure of access to the deliberations either directly or indirectly through representatives. And, as noted, it upholds the constraint imposed on those charged with responsibility to seek the common good, that if their performance is unsatisfactory, they will not always be returned to office – depending on the election results.

Democracy is not without its flaws in this respect, however, since the necessary consideration of every democratically elected politician is whether or not their preferred policy will diminish or increase their chances of being re-elected. This short-term focus on the next election can distract considerably from the long-term issues that affect justice to future generations. Older citizens seem more likely to vote than the younger generation with the result that short-term measures designed to pacify current voters can unintentionally be at the expense of future taxpayers. Democratic processes have this disadvantage of permitting the long-term perspective to be neglected in favour of the short-term, and burdens to be laid on future generations to the benefit of the present. Deficit budgeting, for one, has this effect, and the pain suffered by many in these islands and in Europe as a whole through recent austerity policies testifies to democracy's weakness.

Another possible weakness is conditioned by the actual structures in place. Where those structures militate against the formation of stable governments the very purpose of democracy can be frustrated, namely, the making of decisions in the absence of consensus. Where some decision has to be taken, but there is no assured majority for a government in congress or parliament, then the government is hamstrung and unable to take decisions. The great advantage of proportional representation is that it increases the representation of all streams of opinion among the electorate but its disadvantage is that it can undermine the creation of a viable majority in the chamber. This has become evident in Ireland.

There is no doubt that the structures of democratic governance belong among the conditions for flourishing, which the Second Vatican Council in its Pastoral Constitution, *Gaudium et Spes*, identifies as the common good in political and social contexts: 'The common good embraces the sum total of all those conditions of social life which enable individuals, families, and organisations to achieve complete and effective fulfilment' (*GS*, 74).

Chapter Nine
Education as Common Good

What are we to make of the reported similarities between the Brexit vote and the American presidential election? Donald Trump had been correct in this respect, that the outcome of the presidential race would be as surprising and as unanticipated as the Brexit result in the UK. He forecast that the polls would be misled in the USA as they had been in the UK. Analysts looking at the breakdown of the vote commented on a number of similarities. In both cases there seems to be a generational divide, as well as an educational gap. These two are linked, no doubt, as the younger generations were the beneficiaries of increased access to education in recent decades. Those with lower levels of educational attainment had tended to vote for Brexit in the UK, and for Donal Trump as president in the USA. College graduates in the UK were more inclined to see the advantages for themselves in the European context and so were more likely to vote to remain in the EU. In the US election, 58 per cent of voters with a postgraduate qualification supported Clinton; while 37 per cent supported Trump. The spread was not so great at the level of college graduates: 49 per cent supported the Democratic candidate; 45 per cent supported the Republican.

How should we interpret this discrepancy, and what implications does it have for educational policy? Evidently, different stories could be constructed to account for the split. One spin says that the more educated voters had the intellectual resources and knowledge to identify and dismiss hype and bluster, and to assess policy and character instead. The conclusion of this account is the regrettable one that ignorance, prejudice and fear won the day. The alternative spin is to discount the claims of the educated as somehow self-authenticating and to see college qualification as giving access to an elite group in society which for a long time has been able to manipulate the levers of influence to gain advantage for itself. The conclusion from this version is that the excluded, ignored and discounted class of blue collar and service workers as well as the unemployed have finally had enough and demanded that their concerns be taken seriously by government.

This view might seem very black and white, but it doesn't have to be either-or: it can be both-and. Though whichever story we prefer, there remains a serious question to be addressed about the role played by our educational systems in the construction of the political culture. Do our educational institutions contribute to a division in society or do they help to foster harmony? Does education contribute to the common good? Does educational attainment lead to a privileged elite and so divide the successful from the failures? In the presence of so many centrifugal forces pulling society apart, shouldn't education be a counter-influence, and not another source of division?

This is not a new question in the Irish context. There has been a long-running debate about the divisiveness of maintaining fee-paying schools and the resultant consolidation of a social and economic elite in society. I don't enter that debate here, but suggest that the issues can be better addressed if we consider the different ways in which education is a good, and in particular, how education can be considered a common good. I attempt to clarify some of the important terms needed for the discussion, and show how education can be considered as a private good, a public good, a club good, and a common good. Private, public and club goods are technical terms from economics which will be explained below.

The debates about education in Ireland are different to those in the UK, but the language for dealing with the basic issues is common to both. In Ireland at present the main focus is on primary and secondary education, while the major innovations in UK educational policy are in third level. Not exclusively, of course, since the trend to create academies and free schools and to remove second level schools from local political control reflects the same agenda as is found in third level education. The difference between the two countries is not such as to preclude comparison. Inevitably, what becomes standard at third level impacts on secondary and primary education since these prepare candidates to move on to the higher level. And given the pressures of international comparison for universities we can expect that the Irish universities will not remain unaffected by the British experience, and Irish secondary education will be required to adapt.

The key policy innovation in third level education in the UK is the marketisation of education. Other inherited communal assets are also being marketised: what formerly were deemed public goods in the UK are now being treated as private goods, in the cases of public transport, water supply and, to some extent, medical care, social welfare and even the prison service. Just as the UK government has privatised these, so it is attempting to privatise third level education. The key question, then, is whether it is better for the common good that education be regarded primarily as a private good, or primarily as a public good?

The marketisation of higher education, driven not actually by the supposed market but by governments and regulative agencies, imposes on our colleges and universities the need to attend to league tables, audits, and research evaluation exercises. Prospective students and their parents demand data on retention rates, passing rates and honours achievements, employment and further career achievements of graduates, as well as basic information about the courses and programmes of studies. The customer must be provided with all relevant information before making a choice to purchase. This is the dominant model, transferred to educational systems from the world of business and, in particular, consumer protection legislation. The prospective student is a customer, prepared to lay out a lot of money, in fact, now in the UK, to go into debt to do so, in order to purchase an education. The politicians driving the changes are interested in efficiency, and no doubt that is a value. Efficiency should mean less wastage, and more effective application of resources to needs. But other values are harmed or lost in the process so that the policy is in danger of being counterproductive. The problem lies in the assumption that competitive markets are the only way to achieve the required efficiency, granted their proven success in doing so in some commercial contexts.

In education, the drive to introduce competitive markets to achieve better performance and more efficient use of resources has had and will continue to have disastrous consequences.

One trivial consequence is in the changed attitude of students. They calculate the number of lectures they receive in a year and divide the annual fee by that number to inform the professors that each lecture is costing each student from £50 to £120, depending on the course. And they demand value for money. Of course their calculations are ridiculous, but that's not the point; the students are being conditioned into an attitude of entitlement, whereby they as consumers are protected by legislation from being deceived by misdescription or false information, or substandard products. And since they pay for the lecture they assume they are free to attend or not as it suits. And as customers they know the adage that 'the customer is always right'.

More a cause for concern is the way that universities and faculty are being conditioned into thinking of themselves analogously as providers of goods and services in a market in which their survival depends on their success in satisfying customers. So the academic providers conform to the trend and speak uncritically of their programmes and courses as 'products', and they themselves as producers and providers. It seems harmless enough, and also seems to fit with what is definitely part of the experience – students pay fees for the courses they attend, and universities rely on those fees and other income sources to meet their costs and invest in development and expansion. Recruitment relies more and more on 'marketing' departments borrowing skills and practices from the commercial world, and these encourage us to formulate our mission statements with an eye to recruitment, ensuring that we highlight our unique selling points (USPs). Of course they want us to acknowledge that we are in the market to sell something, so that by doing so we will become more successful, in market share, and revenues.

And as we *buy* into this way of thinking of ourselves as 'sellers' (note how easily the metaphor of buying slipped in here) so we become conditioned more and more to interpret our experience and options in terms of this marketing model.

Market failure is the usual context for the introduction of the notion of public goods. 'Public good' is a technical term in economics, and is not identical with common good. Market failure refers to those goods or services that cannot be supplied via the market, because no entrepreneur can undertake the cost of supplying the good when there is no assurance that beneficiaries will pay. Who will provide street lighting by way of the market when people can enjoy the benefit of the lighting once it is in place without having to pay? The market will not deliver this good, so we rely on public authority to provide it. It recovers payment for this and other services (defence, justice, etc.) via taxation, and not by means of quid pro quo payments in exchange for each usage. Public goods are non-excludable (once they are in place it is not possible to exclude some categories of people – everybody sees the traffic lights, even those driving untaxed cars) and non-rivalrous (adding more people to the enjoyment does not diminish the benefits of those already included). By contrast, private goods are both excludable and rivalrous. In between there is a spectrum, including the categories of commons and club goods.

In several ways, of course, education is a private good. The certificate obtained at the end of the course is definitely private, with the graduate's name printed on it; the school or college place is private, especially where there is scarcity or quotas. These are excludable and rivalrous goods. This is the aspect which attracts the attention of state administration – achieve efficiency by encouraging the market in the goods – places on courses and qualifications at the end. And a market requires competition, so the state has encouraged private enterprises to enter the market in the expectation that the newcomers by offering students attractive alternatives, will oblige the existing universities to up their game.

As well as being a private good, in other respects education is also a club good: it introduces the student into a network of contacts. Once graduated a student can rely on the support and patronage of fellow alumni. A club good is excludable, but non-rivalrous. Others not from the same school can be excluded from the preferential treatment, but the inclusion of others from the same school is non-rivalrous and hence tolerable, since no individual is disadvantaged. One of the ongoing concerns of educators and the challenge of the recent experience of voting patterns in the UK and the USA is the extent to which we are creating club goods. Are we reinforcing the elite as a distinctive section of society? Is higher education a ticket to social advantage from which others are excluded? Definitely not a common good, therefore, on the criterion elaborated above, that anything which systematically excludes from a share in the good for the sake of which we cooperate could not be a common good.

But before considering education as a common good, we still have to clarify education as a public good. When levels of literacy, numeracy and oracy (the ability to express oneself eloquently in speech) in a society are high, when the electorate in a democracy is capable of discerning issues of policy and exercising critical judgement about candidates and their programmes, when print and broadcast media carry a quality of debate about relevant issues that goes beyond sloganeering and name-calling, then we see the benefit of education as a public good. Once it is in place, all people benefit, and no one is disadvantaged by the addition of further participants to the enjoyment of this quality of public life. The latter must be qualified, of course, by the condition that the new additions bring a comparable capacity and are prepared to engage in public life on the terms on which they are admitted.

Education is a public good, a shared asset, when relatively high levels of literacy and numeracy and competence for engagement in political discourse are widespread in society facilitating respectful and open debate on controversial issues. But when we observe the potential divisiveness of educational attainment in our political communities we have reason to doubt that education is a shared asset. The similarity in voting patterns in the UK and USA experiences suggest that education may be functioning not as a public good, and therefore a real asset to common life, but as a club good reinforcing the advantages of an elite.

Another way in which education can and ought to be a public good is related to the achievements of the rule of law. The rule of law itself is also a public good in being non-excludable and non-rivalrous: once in place it is there for everyone and no one can be disadvantaged just because others are treated according to the law. A relatively high level of education in a populace is a fundamental precondition for the rule of law. Public officials in their various roles and capacities will not do justice unless they are sufficiently skilled and competent, and sensitive to the obligations arising from the human rights of the people with whom they have to deal. Without the capacity to imagine themselves in the position of the other, to think their way into the mindset of peoples from other cultures and traditions, citizens in our world will be unable to deal with the challenges posed by the presence of a great variety of cultures and religions. In this sense too education is a public good.

With the shift to privatisation, our societies are being subjected to a vast social experiment in which students and universities are being conditioned into the attitudes of the marketplace. It is not the skills of citizenship, of neighbourliness, of dialogue partners, which are valued above all, but the marketable skills, transferable skills, which make one a valued commodity in the labour market, that students and their parents pursue. The values of service, the sense of obligation to benefit those less well off, the duty to put one's privileged assets to use for the good of others, are undermined by the reinforced attitude that the education has been paid for. It is property, a possession, a private good, to be used or exercised at the whim of the owner. Students will exaggeratedly claim to have earned their degree through their own hard work, not attending to the many social contributions to their advancement for which no payment has been made. Here too an economic term can highlight the dimensions that are not taken into account. In the maintenance of any education system there are 'externalities', costs borne by some of the stakeholders that are not compensated in the market. It is irrelevant to the economic consideration that those costs are willingly borne by educators, such as the religious men and women who built the Irish educational system and other dedicated educators. The volunteering by parents and others who provide support for extracurricular activities, including sport, is another externality that is not monetarised. The marketing of education as a private good privileges the economic attitude to understanding education and in that mindset certain elements such as externalities do not appear, and hence are likely to be overlooked and forgotten. A culture of education provision is being fostered that will be unable to sustain our inherited institutions of education which have relied on very different values: the values of service, the sense of obligation to benefit those less well off, the duty to put one's privileged assets to use for the good of others, are undermined by the reinforced attitude that education is a private property purchased on the market.

These are the ways in which we can speak of education as a public good. In what way is it a common good? There are two cases: practical and ontic. The practical sense is that wherever people cooperate for some good, they have a good in common, a common good. That good in common that we strive for together in the practical sense might be one or all of the different kinds of good. Our common good might be a private good (qualifications for our children); it could be a club good (networks for UCD alumni); or it could be a public good (high levels of educational attainment conditioning political discourse and widespread respect for the rule of law). We can reformulate this point in terms of human rights as discussed above in chapter seven. My legal team and I might cooperate in pursuing as our common good a specific private good, the vindication of my right not to be discriminated against in employment. With my fellow trades union members we might have a club good as our common good, for which we cooperate, for example, in securing recognition for our particular situation as occasional lecturers. With my fellow academics dedicated to researching and teaching about the regime of human rights our common good could be the public good of increased and widespread public awareness of and commitment to maintaining the regime of human rights, an integral part of the rule of law.

Perhaps the more important way in which education is a common good is the ontic sense of good. As a completion or fulfilment of individuals and communities education enables them to *be* more and to realise to a greater extent their human potential. What fulfils people is for their good, enabling them to flourish. Education is not narrowly limited to academic achievement, of course, but also includes personal formation and empowerment for relationship of all kinds, including the political friendship of citizenship, and so as contributing to human flourishing in the fullest sense it deserves to be part of the practical common good, that which we deliberately name as the point of our cooperation.

The American classical philosopher Martha Nussbaum is an ally on these concerns, and articulates the vision of education's goal from a Stoic perspective. Her book title, *Cultivating Humanity*, is borrowed from Seneca. She sees the need to defend education in the humanities and to defend values threatened by the encroachment of economistic calculations.[1] Her focus is classical, namely, the role of education in producing citizens who are capable of participating in a richly diverse society and political system. The products of university education are not the programmes and degrees, but citizens, and, therefore, the most fundamental question in specifying the purpose of education is to identify what the good citizen in the present day should be and should know. Diversity of culture and background and lifestyle characterises the contemporary world. To be capable of contributing to handling the kinds of problems that arise in this

---

1 Martha Nussbaum, *Cultivating Humanity: A Classical Defense of Reform in Liberal Education*, Cambridge, Mass.: Harvard University Press, 1997; Martha Nussbaum, *Not for Profit: Why Democracy Needs the Humanities*, Princeton, N.J.: Princeton University Press, 2010.

world of differences requires capacities for dialogue in search of intelligent cooperative solutions. Cultivation of these capacities is the aim of a liberal, as distinct from a technical or vocational, education. Nussbaum subscribes to the Stoic ideal of the 'world citizen' and the 'cultivation of humanity' as the aim of liberal education. She lists three capacities that are essential.

The first is the capacity for critical examination of oneself and one's traditions, so that one can live the examined life in Socrates's sense. This means the ability to subject inherited meanings and values and authorities to critical review. Critical review does not mean rejection necessarily, but that citizens can own their own identity and represent it with conviction.

A second ability is the capacity to understand oneself as sharing a common humanity with all other men and women. While local identity and loyalty is easily known and expressed, it requires a deliberate process of education to inculcate the awareness of a solidarity with others of differing racial and national backgrounds, religious affiliation, and with other differences, including gender and sexuality.

Narrative imagination is the third ability: the ability to think and imagine oneself in the place of another, and to understand the emotions and wishes and desires of those very different from ourselves. Nussbaum acknowledges that these three abilities do not exhaust the requirements for intelligent citizenship, but they are central to the role to be played by a liberal education in preparing citizens for today's world.

If people are to be capable of acting as responsible partners in a very complex world, they must have learned to live alongside differences of many kinds. They must have learned to understand themselves and their traditions as situated in a plural and interdependent world. This means that they must be capable of operating at two levels: they must be comfortable in their own tradition and be at home with their distinctive identity; on the other hand, they must be capable of meeting others from differing backgrounds in the public forum on a basis of understanding, respect and tolerance. There is a tendency to regard the public forum only as a market place or bargaining table, where different interest groups meet in order to compete for power. Of course, the competitive nature of interest-group politics cannot be denied and must be allowed its place. But this form of politics alone will not serve the common good. For that a form of encounter must be possible in which despite their differences people can encounter one another as world citizens.

Debate and dialogue is contrasted with bargaining and deal-making. It presupposes a commitment to fostering an alternative space for political engagement than the competition for power in forms in which the stronger (more passionate, more numerous, more resourced, better organised and mobilised) is sure to win.

Nussbaum addresses religiously affiliated schools and colleges, acknowledging their dual mission: 'advancing higher education in a pluralistic democracy, and perpetuating their specific traditions'. Her argument is that both tasks can be fulfilled and that for both to be done well the three essentials of world citizenship must be present. The cultivation of understanding and tolerance for diversity, which is essential to the education of the world citizen is not necessarily to the detriment of local and particular identity. Rather, the sense of solidarity with others based on common humanity merely means that one must accept limits in the name of reason and humanity to what one would do in the name of some local or particular loyalty.

The goal of producing world citizens is profoundly opposed to the spirit of identity politics, which holds that one's primary affiliation is with one's local group, whether national or religious or ethnic or based on sexuality or gender. This is a frequently reiterated theme in her book:

> [W]e need not give up our special affections and identifications, whether national or ethnic or religious; but we should work to make all human beings part of our community of dialogue and concern, showing respect for the human wherever it occurs, and allowing that respect to constrain our national or local politics.[2]

In *Not for Profit*, Nussbaum is concerned about the pressures to consider and evaluate university education in economic categories. Her point throughout is not that a concern for the economy and a business culture should be replaced with a focus on the personal development of citizens. It is not a case of 'either-or', but of 'both-and'. The mistake of current trends throughout the world is not that technology and business are being fostered, but that a liberal arts education is being neglected. One is promoted at the expense of the other. And where cuts are being made in some universities religious studies departments appear more expendable, since they are not viewed as being important. But for Nussbaum, the study of religion belongs at the core of the humanities and should be part of the education for world citizenship that she advocates. Given her emphasis on the three dimensions of education for citizenship – the ability to be self-critical, an understanding of

---

2   Nussbaum, *Cultivating Humanity*, pp. 60–61.

a common humanity across cultures different to one's own, and the capacity to enter imaginatively into the life experience and aspirations of another – the relevance of the religious studies is constantly repeated.

Education for citizenship, understood as participation in politics, is not achieved by the completion of a course on civics but requires a greater commitment of resources by a political community. It must belong to the common good of such a society to have a well-functioning liberal education, including religious studies, because it also belongs to the common good of such a society that education be a public good, a shared resource sustaining a certain quality of political discourse and public debate about policy.

Chapter Ten
The European Union and the Common Good

A major split threatens the European Union. The coincidence of two significant events is creating the perfect storm. On the one hand is Brexit, and on the other hand is the influx of migrants arriving on the EU's southern shores in Greece, Sicily, Malta, and to a lesser extent Spain. These two challenges together have opened up a chasm that threatens to lead to a disintegration of the EU. The continuing inertia of the member states along with their inability to develop and implement an agreed policy for the treatment of the migrant crisis reveals a major weakness at the heart of the EU. There seem to be three different positions: those member states like Greece, Italy and Malta who bear the brunt of the work of coping with arriving migrants; member states with Germany to the fore who argue for solidarity among the members in sharing the burden of welcoming migrants; and other member states whose willingness to receive and integrate the migrants is severely restricted. The last group is encouraged by the success of the Brexit campaign in the UK. It demonstrates the power of populist campaigning focused solely on securing national interests. Various popular and nationalist groups within member states, including France and Germany, are hoping for success in national elections such as the presidential election in France, and this adds an extra pressure blocking a resolution of the migrant crisis.

The migrant crisis is not the first to pose a challenge to the existence of the Union. The rapid expansion of the Union to its present size of twenty-eight members; the debates about a constitution for the EU; the banking crisis following the 2007 implosion; the Euro and sovereign debt crisis and, in particular, the Greek problem, have all posed challenges to the identity and the survival of the EU. The present crisis, however, seems to pose more of a threat because the UK example highlights the real practical possibility of withdrawal – even if it is not at all clear what withdrawal will entail.

The crisis is real and politicians and commentators are busy trying to make sense of it. One way in which they do so is to pose the question whether the Union is founded on shared values, or on shared interests. In one sense the distinction used here is clear and also plausible. Peoples might be united in sharing the values of respect for human rights, solidarity with the unfortunate and marginalised, commitment to the rule of law and to international justice. With these values in common, the peoples of the EU potentially share a bond of unity that is strong enough to sustain the Union through its occasional crises. And where the bond of unity proves not to be strong enough to hold against pressure, the supposed agreement on values is exposed as groundless.

On the other hand, the EU can be seen as drawing peoples together whose interests are furthered by cooperation. Here the principal image is not of a community united in sharing value commitments, but of a marketplace, in which many participants find it convenient for their purposes to cooperate with others. Each one has an interest in getting a bargain, buying or selling at a price that gives the purchaser value for money and the seller a return on investment with something to spare. An agreed exchange allows each one to do well, without having to consider how well the others fare. The interests each one brings to the exchange are different, but the cooperation in the market place allows these different interests to be satisfied at the same time. For many commentators, pointing to the origins of the EU in the coal and steel agreements and the common market, the Union is fundamentally grounded in the pursuit of interests whose representatives happen to find it convenient to collaborate in market-like structures.

For these commentators, there cannot be any point in continuing to collaborate when the interests motivating the cooperation cannot be satisfied. Crises for the Union arise when individual peoples or their representatives find that their particular interests are not sufficiently catered for in the collaboration. The Brexit arguments are a case in point. The voters of the UK, persuaded by some of their political representatives, have decided to withdraw from the EU in order to protect their interests, which they judge to have been neglected by EU policies. Chief among these declared interests are the elements of sovereignty, which include control of borders, control of immigration, and control of domestic legislation.

The highlighting of national interest achieved by the Brexit campaign and vote has found an echo in other countries of the Union, in which local and national interests are newly championed. Polish leaders speak of the interest in preserving the integrity of the national culture, which they see as threatened by the inclusion of large numbers of Muslims. Hungary's leaders similarly wish to sustain a path of national development for which EU membership was convenient but which should not be allowed place demands jeopardising that development. At the forefront of the pressure from migration both Greece and Italy, as well as Malta, see the burden on their economies and administrative systems as stretching these to breaking point and so they protest the urgent need for a broader system of support from partner countries in the EU. So many different interests being championed in these debates lend weight to the view that the Union is not based on shared values, but is founded on shared interests, and when common interests cannot be found then the relevance of the EU is questionable and its survival is uncertain.

'Deals and ideals' is a parallel pair of terms to that of 'interests and values'. Any casual observer of European affairs must be struck by the continual pursuit of a deal. Even in hoping to ward off a defeat in the EU referendum the then Prime Minister David Cameron attempted to negotiate a deal with regard to the welfare rights of migrant workers and other matters. A special deal for the UK, he thought, would demonstrate to voters that their interests could be adequately protected within the EU. The UK not least under the leadership of Margaret Thatcher had been very successful in negotiating special treatment for itself, in the rebate on its contributions, exemption from some elements of the social charter, acceptance of privileged access of commonwealth countries to the UK market, and independent border control. The deals have been done because the EU member states have wanted the UK to remain in the Union.

Ireland too has been particularly successful in EU negotiations, and our politicians and special interest lobbyists have mastered the skills of working the system in Brussels and Strasbourg. Whether on behalf of Irish farmers or the fishing industry, or for the sake of infrastructural investment from the regional development or structural funds, our Irish representatives have not been slow to seek a deal in Europe to benefit the country. So much has Brussels become a focal point for lobbyists from all countries and interests that critics of the EU point to this fact as evidence of what is called the democratic deficit, the situation where important decisions are made, not by elected representatives, but by the Commission and its officials in Brussels. That is an important challenge, but I don't want to reflect further on it here. The central role of deal-making in the business of Europe is my focus, and the impression that the Union is about such deals, and not about ideals. The ideals usually invoked in terms of solidarity, equality of participation, human rights and the rule of law are always mentioned in the speeches of politicians and in the preambles to treaties and agreements, but when it comes down to it, it is alleged, the deals are not driven by the ideals, and the ideals may have to be overlooked or ignored at times to ensure that a deal is done. So it seems plausible to use this pair of concepts, deals or ideals, in commenting on the reality of the European Union today.

Interests, not values; deals, not ideals. Is it really so? Do we have to accept the validity of first impressions and the commentaries of observers? There is a Catholic standpoint that says: 'No! We don't have to see it this way.' Without denying the usefulness of such distinctions between interests and values, and between deals and ideals, the Catholic world view rejects the proposition that these, while distinguishable, can be separated. Wherever there are interests, there are also values in play, wherever people make deals, there are ideals at stake. The Catholic attitude refuses to allow values to be divorced from the messy, nitty-gritty of interests. We can see the truth of this on both a small scale and a broad canvas.

On the broad canvas is the range of Catholic doctrine in which we see many elements where the divine, the holy and the transcendent is understood to be immanent in material and bodily reality. The teaching on the Incarnation, that God in Jesus Christ has become human and part of human history, and that Jesus continues to be present in the stuff of this world, whether in the bread and wine of the Eucharist, in the words of forgiveness and absolution, in the anointing of the sick, or in the marital relationship of Christian couples, lends depth and mystery to the fundamental conviction that these realities, these values, make sense of our everyday reality. The result is that in the Catholic world view we never expect to find interests separable from values. There are always values at stake in both senses of value. Either values such as life or friendship – making sense of our goals, or values such as fidelity or justice – setting standards for our actions.

This applies to such realities as the EU, and whether it is to be understood solely in terms of interests, or in terms of values. The Catholic response is to say that it cannot be either-or, but that values are always at stake in the interests people pursue. The interests that individuals and peoples together pursue are in good things: a quality of life ensuring a measure of comfort and security, confidence in the rule of law and the protection of rights, and fundamental freedoms of conscience, speech and assembly. It is not a helpful strategy to counter the Brexiteers or the Polish politicians by relying on a simple disjunction between interests and values. There has to be a real engagement with the values driving the policy, and that requires a sympathetic attempt to understand those values and why they are important to the proponents. Those values must help us understand the real interests of people and why they are motivated by them. Independence, national autonomy, sovereign control of a country's destiny are genuine values, even if they are in tension with other values such as international cooperation, solidarity in addressing common problems and the institutionalisation of human rights at a global level.

Nussbaum's recommendations on what is required for the education of citizens of the world outlined in the previous chapter are applicable also to nations and peoples who need to have the imaginative capacity to enter into the situation of others. This will safeguard against an abstract consideration of values remote from the genuine concerns of people today. When we consider such traditional EU values as solidarity and subsidiarity, human dignity and equality, we will have to locate them in the lived experience of people, and not just in the high-powered language of speeches and preambles.

However, the urgency of interests, especially when threatened, makes clear how important it is for our shared political culture to sustain the awareness of the ideals and values at stake. This is a responsibility not only for educators, but especially for political leaders, to ensure that the electorate is literate in the values for the sake of which the institutions are created and maintained. The Brexit decision did not arise out of thin air: it was the result of decades of neglect by the political establishment in the UK that had never seriously engaged with the positive values of the EU. The terms of the debate were formulated in prognoses of costs and benefits of the alternatives of staying or leaving the Union. Were the reasons for belonging only ever economic?

The typical rhetoric of British politicians has been exclusively about 'what is best for Britain'. Just as we have educated people in sciences and technology and neglected to educate and form them in citizenship, politics, and religion, so our political leaders have neglected to form the political culture in which a reasonable debate about membership of the EU can take place.

In the Brexit debate many of those who in the context of the Scottish referendum argued for the maintenance of the Union subsequently argued for withdrawal from the EU. This is curious, because the arguments made in terms of distance from Brussels, lack of control or influence over what is decided in Brussels, and the inefficiencies associated with additional layers of bureaucracy, all intended to support a leave decision, were precisely parallel to the arguments made by Scottish Nationalists considering London, not Brussels, as the remote bureaucratic and indifferent capital. Why couldn't the same arguments offered to the Scottish Nationalists in support of the Union of the United Kingdom also serve in support of the European Union?

Slogans like 'We are Stronger Together' come to mind. But what do they mean? What are the reasons behind the slogans? Among the possible reasons are the following: we have responsibilities, and we need appropriate institutions to exercise our responsibilities and achieve worthwhile objectives. While the institutions of the EU may not be perfect, they are intended for this purpose. These ideas can be summarised in the notions of solidarity and subsidiarity.

With the notion of solidarity we are reminded that our common humanity, our interdependence, and our knowledge of the plight of our neighbours oblige us to take steps to deal with the problems that affect them. To act effectively we need appropriate institutions at different levels, global (UN) and regional or continental (EU). Some may deny that we have responsibilities for others. Ethicists identify for us the grounds of obligation. If there is someone in need; if you have the capacity to do something about it; and if you are nearby, then you have responsibility to act. Need, capacity and proximity make you responsible.

The fact that the EU would be very much weaker without the presence of the UK and so its capacity to deal with issues would be diminished if Britain were to leave the EU could have raised questions of responsibility for sustaining and not undermining the common effort of the EU. That a vote to leave might be a shirking of responsibility was never admitted. Responsibility for what? NATO offers an interesting comparison. The purpose of NATO from its foundation has been to offer security to Europe in the face of the threat of the Warsaw Pact, and now more recently a resurgent Russian Federation. The USA has been a leading player in NATO and has underwritten the commitment to European security. The USA might well have decided to leave Europe to its fate. After all, why should its taxpayers (always reluctant) continue to contribute to the security of Europe? We in Europe have perhaps taken it for granted that they should and have not been too scrupulous in offering our thanks. This applies also to Ireland, which has been able to shelter under this security umbrella while protesting its neutrality. The USA is an example of a country accepting a responsibility and bearing the costs associated with it for the sake of benefits that accrue primarily to others as well as benefits to itself. This example might be emulated, but there is little chance of that happening while politicians only ever argue in terms of costs and pay-off.

In contrast to NATO, focused on security, the EU is focused on a much wider range of needs and capacities. These also include security, given the ancestry of the Union in the rebuilding of relationships between countries and nations that had been bitter enemies for centuries. 1870, 1914, 1939: within a span of only seventy years Germany and France had been three times in a vicious war. That is the headline example, but other countries can be named too. Italy and Germany in the Spanish Civil War, Poland and Czechoslovakia as victims of Nazi Germany, and recently the turmoil in the Balkans following the disintegration of Yugoslavia. Very much aware of the dangers of war and the associated consequences, those who created the European Union have worked to build safeguards against war by fostering collaboration in structures of shared responsibility. As a member of the EU, Britain is obliged to play its part in exercising that responsibility. The decision to leave was a declaration of unwillingness to be responsible, along with others, for the maintenance of a common good: the peace we take for granted. NATO is one instrument for security, an explicitly military one. However, there is a less tangible but even more important bulwark against war in the bonds of solidarity and the cultivation of familiarity with each other and one another's problems, and the collaboration in institutions that are designed to address those problems. Perhaps it is more accurate to say that the decision to withdraw from the EU was a decision to give priority to values of sovereignty, national autonomy and control of immigration, over those of solidarity with neighbours. But the effect is the same: the relinquishing of responsibility.

Whether on a national or an international scale, institutions are problems as well as solutions. Healthcare, education, prisons, welfare, are all focus of conflict and continual demand for improvement. If our national institutions exhibit crises, we do not expect to solve the problems by abandoning the institutions, but we recognise the need to reform and improve them. That the European institutions have flaws and are inefficient and overly bureaucratic should not surprise us. As in the domestic case, reform and improvement are required, and it is there that responsibility is to be exercised. Interestingly, the EU articulates among its values the principle of subsidiarity, a principle which provides ammunition for those who wish to reform the institutions. This principle means that responsibility for taking action should be located at the lowest possible level in a hierarchically structured organisation. A distorted form of this has been implemented in the UK when central government has devolved to local government the responsibility for deciding what cuts in services and welfare provision are to be made, while deciding centrally what resources are to be made available. Proper subsidiarity should allow for the raising of revenue at the local level as well, something the EU does, and the UK does not, and neither does Ireland since the fateful elimination of local rates. The role of central government, according to the principle of subsidiarity, is to support and assist the agencies that are as close to the ground and to the beneficiaries as possible. Reform and improvement can invoke this value of subsidiarity as well as that of solidarity.

The needs which motivate the collaboration of the state members of the EU go beyond security. Inequalities in life's opportunities for education and employment, inequalities in standards of living, inequalities in health provision and other infrastructures, have called forth a sharing of responsibility to help one another. While the European project is built on support for a market economy, it has always wanted to avoid fostering the kind of competitiveness that would allow each member to look after its own interests exclusively, and 'let the devil take the hindmost'. The endorsement of social capitalism in the EU has wanted to see the market-driven economy as an instrument for other common goods, which we usually summarise as well-being, welfare or flourishing. An economy which allows some to founder without support, which can tolerate the exclusion of some from participation and from benefiting from wealth creation is foreign to the European ideal. This has been the value at the heart of the common agricultural policy (CAP) ensuring we did not foster a destructive competitiveness among our agricultural sectors but guaranteed a viable basis for traditional ways of life. The ideal has been a noble one. The institutions and arrangements have not always been successful, having unintended consequences, as for instance the closure of food markets to African producers, and the destruction of some African markets by dumping subsidised produce against which local producers could not compete. But the commitment to addressing inequalities has meant that wealthier and stronger countries have been willing to support measures to help weaker and poorer regions and states to catch up. This ambition to tackle inequality is still worth supporting, all the more so in a world which is growing more unequal.

The European Union has been an important agency for reinforcing commitment to human rights and the rule of law. Nowadays the rule of law entails recognition and respect for the rights of everyone, without discrimination on arbitrary grounds. Within Europe the EU with its institutions is not the only forum for the maintenance and promotion of rights, although it has been significant in developing the rights of workers. The European

Convention on Human Rights with its Court of Human Rights is another, for the creation of which Winston Churchill shares considerable responsibility. He saw respect for human rights and their enforcement through appropriate instruments as essential to safeguarding against a recurrence of the crimes against persons associated with totalitarian regimes. What is worrying about the increased emphasis on local issues and national interests is that it seems to imply an abandonment of the willingness to accept responsibility for a shared culture in Europe based on respect for the rule of law, a common good. There is no discussion of how those responsibilities might otherwise be exercised. The institutions in place are there for this purpose, even if they are inadequate and in need of reform and adjustment. All of our peoples in Europe share this responsibility.

The lack of depth in the discussion of some of these themes, in particular the UK's responsibility as a state for the maintenance of a quality of relations between neighbouring states and in the global context, reflects the absence of awareness of the values that have motivated the creation and maintenance of the European Union. That absence is due to the neglect of the political culture and political leaders to explain why membership of the Union is also 'Best for Europe as well as being Best for Britain'. It is due to the illiteracy about our common goods, which include these values listed above: a culture of shared responsibility, the rule of law, familiarity with each other in our differences, relationships that are friendly and conducive to cooperation, concern for the victims and the excluded, willingness to bear costs which benefit all, and not primarily ourselves.

There are values and ideals at stake in the current turmoil of European politics. Those values belong to the common good of the EU, and it is also a common good of European citizens that understanding of and commitment to those values be strengthened. This book, hopefully, contributes to that task.

Conclusion

As has been emphasised at several points in this exploration, there is no implication that because something is declared to be good that there is an obligation to pursue it. The hope in writing the book is that as people are made more aware of what is involved in the goods they share with others and the conditions on which they rely for their pursuit of their chosen goods they will become committed to securing and maintaining their common goods. The discussion hopes to have shown how the good attracts – think of our enjoyment of friends' company as we share an entertaining story – and so it relies on the attractiveness of the goods at stake in our common life. There is no attempt at moralising and imposing obligations on people.

The discussion has attempted to show how any imposition as such is contrary to the spirit and nature of common goods, as articulated in the two criteria. Both these criteria are grounded in philosophical analysis as well as in the tradition of Catholic social thought. The first criterion stresses that any proposal which systematically excludes persons or groups from a share in the enjoyment of the goods we pursue together cannot claim to be for the common good. The second criterion opposes reductionism or selectivity in accounting for human well-being. Any proposal that systematically excludes from consideration any dimension of well-being as underserving of attention in our collaborative efforts cannot claim to be for the common good. The operation of these criteria in practice through history allows us to understand the dynamic of overcoming discrimination and exclusion, leading to the institutionalisation of human rights. The rationale of the second criterion is operative, for instance, in the expansion of human rights discourse from civil and political rights to social and economic.

The parallel formulations in CST succinctly specify the common good as the integral fulfilment of every person and of the whole person, drawing on the words of Pope Paul VI. The stress on the whole person declares resistance to any reduction of the person to just one element, as for instance seeing the worker as merely a cost of production in the economy. The principle of subsidiarity also echoes this resistance to reductionism, insisting that persons not be deprived of their autonomy, their freedom to choose their own good and to work themselves to attain it. Protecting autonomy upholds the entirety of the person, ensuring that provision for welfare in terms of basic material needs not be allowed override respect for the person who must always be a partner in the effort. As the integral fulfilment of the whole person echoes the second criterion, the integral fulfilment of every person echoes the first, that none be excluded. Solidarity with those in danger of being excluded or who are actually excluded from the benefits of social cooperation is the parallel principle to subsidiarity in CST. This finds a more insistent formulation in the Church's language when it professes a preferential option for the poor.

Integral fulfilment can find many biblical metaphors such as 'the heavenly banquet', 'the beatific vision', or 'life in the resurrection'. But as metaphors these defy precise description, and point rather to something mysterious, that is desired and striven for. We know that the criteria of the common good will be fully satisfied, but beyond that we must remain content to name what we hope for and live with the vagueness of our understanding. The notion of heuristic has been used for this naming without knowing, in the hope of discovery. It applies also to the social and political collaboration which aims at goals we can loosely name as justice, peace, prosperity for all, security and provision for care. These are our common goods, vaguely formulated, and in their name we institutionalise practices and regimes which are more definite and concrete, and which usually only partly satisfy our aspirations. So the Church has learned to speak of the common good in social and political contexts as the set of conditions that will enable persons and communities to achieve their fulfilment. Among those conditions we have looked at the human rights regime and the rule of law, educational systems, the economy and the role of markets and of property, the institutions of democracy, and at the international level the European Union. All these belong among the conditions we have put in place for supporting a decent human existence, oriented to the fulfilment of every person and of the whole person. In each case, however, there are deficits and failures, and the struggle to mend these or replace institutions with something better is our shared pursuit of common goods.

As a Christian I can understand all this as sharing in the desire of Jesus expressed in his reason for taking on his mission, 'that they may have life, and have it abundantly' (Jn 10:10). I can envisage the collaborative effort in striving for the good and for the good life as both participating in and building up the community of those who ultimately will share the joy of knowing the Father and the Son whom he sent (Jn 17:3). That joy I can only begin to imagine in terms of the most entertaining story I will ever hear in the best company I will ever enjoy.

Bibliography

Aquinas, St Thomas, *Summa Theologiae*, London: Blackfriars, 1963.

Chesterton, G.K., *The Works of G.K. Chesterton*, Ware, Hertfordshire: Wordsworth Poetry Library, 1995, pp. 199–200.

Pontifical Council for Justice and Peace, *Compendium of the Social Doctrine of the Church*, Rome: Libreria Editrice Vaticana, 2004.

Nussbaum, M., *Cultivating Humanity. A Classical Defense of Reform in Liberal Education*, Cambridge, Mass.: Harvard University Press, 1997.

Nussbaum, M., *Not for Profit: Why Democracy Needs the Humanities*, Princeton, N.J.: Princeton University Press, 2010.

Riordan, P., *A Politics of the Common Good*, Dublin: Institute of Public Administration, 1996.

—*A Grammar of the Common Good*, London: Continuum, 2008.

—*Global Ethics and Global Common Goods*, London: Bloomsbury, 2015.

— 'Aristotle and the Politics of the Common Good Today' in N. Sagovsky and P. McGrail (eds), *Together for the Common Good: Towards a National Conversation*, London: SCM Press, 2015, pp. 31–48.

Smith, A., *An Inquiry into the Nature and Causes of the Wealth of Nations*, in two volumes, edited by R.H. Campbell and A.S. Skinner. Indianapolis, Liberty Fund, 1981.

Catholic Social Thought

1891, Pope Leo XIII, *Rerum Novarum*, 'On Capital and Labour', w2.vatican.va/content/leo-xiii/en/encyclicals/documents/ hf_l-xiii_enc_15051891_rerum-novarum.html

1931, Pope Pius XI, *Quadragesimo Anno*, 'On Reconstruction of the Social Order', w2.vatican.va/content/pius-xi/en/ encyclicals/documents/hf_p-xi_enc_19310515_quadragesimo-anno.html

1961, Pope John XXIII, *Mater et Magistra*, 'Mother and Teacher', w2.vatican.va/content/john-xxiii/en/encyclicals/documents/ hf_j-xxiii_enc_15051961_mater.html

1964, Vatican Council II, *Lumen Gentium*, 'Dogmatic Constitution on the Church', www.vatican.va/archive/hist_councils/ii_ vatican_council/documents/vat-ii_const_19641121_lumen-gentium_en.html

1965, Vatican Council II, *Gaudium et Spes*, 'Pastoral Constitution on the Church Today', www.vatican.va/archive/hist_councils/ ii_vatican_council/documents/vat-ii_cons_19651207_ gaudium-et-spes_en.html

1967, Pope Paul VI, *Populorum Progressio*, 'On the Development of Peoples', w2.vatican.va/content/paul-vi/en/encyclicals/documents/hf_p-vi_enc_26031967_populorum.html

1975, Pope Paul VI, *Evangelii Nuntiandi*, 'Pastoral Exhortation on Evangelization', w2.vatican.va/content/paul-vi/en/apost_exhortations/documents/hf_p-vi_exh_19751208_evangelii-nuntiandi.html

1981, Pope John Paul II, *Laborem Exercens*, 'On Human Work', w2.vatican.va/content/john-paul-ii/en/encyclicals/documents/hf_jp-ii_enc_14091981_laborem-exercens.html

1987, Pope John Paul II, *Sollicitudo Rei Socialis*, 'On Social Concern', w2.vatican.va/content/john-paul-ii/en/encyclicals/documents/hf_jp-ii_enc_30121987_sollicitudo-rei-socialis.html

1991, Pope John Paul II, *Centesimus Annus*, 'Centenary', w2.vatican.va/content/john-paul-ii/en/encyclicals/documents/hf_jp-ii_enc_01051991_centesimus-annus.html

2009, Pope Benedict XVI, *Caritas in Veritate*, 'Love in Truth', w2.vatican.va/content/benedict-xvi/en/encyclicals/documents/hf_ben-xvi_enc_20090629_caritas-in-veritate.html

2015, Pope Francis, *Laudato Si'*, 'On Care for Our Common Home', w2.vatican.va/content/francesco/en/encyclicals/documents/papa-francesco_20150524_enciclica-laudato-si.html

Abbreviations

CA: 1991, Pope John Paul II, *Centesimus Annus*, 'Centenary'.

CV: 2009, Pope Benedict XVI, *Caritas in Veritate*, 'Love in Truth'.

EN: 1975, Pope PaulVI, *Evangelii Nuntiandi*, 'Pastoral Exhortation on Evangelisation'.

GS: 1966, Vatican Council II, *Gaudium et Spes*, 'Pastoral Constitution on the Church Today'.

LE: 1981, Pope John Paul II, *Laborem Exercens*, 'On Human Work'.

LG: 1964, Vatican Council II, *Lumen Gentium*, 'Dogmatic Constitution on the Church'.

LS: 2015, Pope Francis, *Laudato Si'*, 'On Care for Our Common Home'.

MM: 1961, Pope John XXIII, *Mater et Magistra*, 'Mother and Teacher'.

PP: 1967, Pope Paul VI, *Populorum Progressio*, 'On the Development of Peoples'.

QA: 1931, Pope Pius XI, *Quadragesimo Anno*, 'On Reconstruction of the Social Order'.

RN: 1891, Pope Leo XIII, *Rerum Novarum*, 'On Capital and Labour'.

SRS: 1987, Pope John Paul II, *Sollicitudo Rei Socialis*, 'On Social Concern'.

May 2005

15th May

We were idling away on the swing seat this afternoon gazing out over the fields and enjoying the warmth of a beautiful spring day. It's been stupendous, not a cloud in the sky, no crop sprayers, Jehovah's Witnesses or neighbouring DIY to send us rushing indoors.

I've never had a garden of my own before and I'm enjoying it. The red kites whistle away up in the sky and all is well with our world – well, all apart from next-door-but-one's rabbit who escaped and has been sneakily chewing my lupin to bits. It's got me fuming and if he is not stopped I fear he's not long for this world – the pot will be set to boil for this particular Harvey if he doesn't watch out. Actually his nickname is Stewart Granger because I couldn't remember James Stewart's name. Same thing though isn't it? I love that film.

We're living in a small but perfectly formed village en route to the Ridgeway in the midst of the Berkshire Downs. The parish is home to people who have lived around these parts all their lives and, nowadays, to 'fancy London types' as well. We only come from a few miles away but are still thought of as foreigners. The nearest station is around a three-mile drive from here and the trains run regularly to Reading and London so it's very easy to commute. Our home is a rented cream-coloured semi-detached ex-council house with a long garden that backs on to waving fields of wheat.